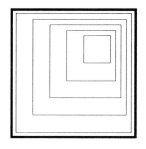

# Review of the Youth Situation, Policies and Programmes in Asia and the Pacific

## United Nations
New York, 1997

ST/ESCAP/1757

| UNITED NATIONS PUBLICATION |
| --- |
| Sales No. E.97.II.F.16 |
| Copyright © United Nations 1997 |
| ISBN: 92-1-119753-8 |

# Contents

Part Two:
Innovative Programmes of Youth Organizations

Part Three:
Report of the Asia-Pacific Meeting on
Human Resources Development for Youth,
22-26 October 1996, Beijing, Including the Beijing Statement
on Human Resources Development for Youth
in Asia and the Pacific

## Tables

## Figures

## Boxes

# Introduction

Youth, as a distinct social group, are defined by the United Nations as persons between the ages of 15 and 24 years. According to that definition, youth constitute approximately one-fifth of the total population of the ESCAP region.

Issues affecting youth received worldwide attention in 1995 with the commemoration by the international community of the tenth anniversary of the International Youth Year: Participation, Development and Peace (1985). A special session of the United Nations General Assembly was convened in 1995 to review issues affecting youth. In concluding its deliberations on the subject, the General Assembly in December 1995 adopted resolution 50/81 containing the World Programme of Action for Youth to the Year 2000 and Beyond. Among the recommendations contained in the World Programme of Action, the General Assembly requested the regional commissions to promote implementation of the Programme through the incorporation of its goals in their plans, through comprehensive reviews of the progress achieved and obstacles encountered, and through identification of the options for further regional action.

In follow-up of the above, the Economic and Social Commission for Asia and the Pacific (ESCAP), adopted in April 1996 resolution 52/4 on "Promoting human resources development among youth in Asia and the Pacific". That resolution called upon ESCAP to convene a regional meeting of senior officials to review human resources development (HRD) policies and programmes for youth and to submit, as background for that meeting, a comprehensive survey of the youth situation and human resources development policies in Asia and the Pacific.

The present publication is presented in compliance with the above-mentioned General Assembly and ESCAP mandates. In preparing this study, the secretariat was guided by the two key instruments which set the basis for all its activities related to youth: the *Jakarta Plan of Action on Human Resources Development in the ESCAP Region*, adopted by the Commission and its forty-fourth session and the *World Programme of Action for Youth to the Year 2000 and Beyond*.

The Jakarta Plan of Action on Human Resources Development was adopted by ESCAP in 1988, the culmination of the deliberations at three consecutive annual sessions of ESCAP on HRD. To reflect the changing needs of the region and to ensure direct imple-mentation of its recommendations by the member Governments, it was subsequently updated in 1994. The Jakarta Plan of Action is based on the principle that people should be recognized as both the principal means and the ultimate end of development. It identifies youth as a priority target group for HRD. The concept of HRD, as advocated in the Jakarta Plan of Action, focuses on three components: (a) investment in human resources; (b) utilization of those human resources; and (c) the participation of human beings in the enjoyment of the benefits of an enhanced quality of life. The Jakarta Plan of Action states that, in all three of these components, the needs and potential of youth must be clearly recognized.

Complementary to the Jakarta Plan of Action, the building blocks of the World Programme of Action for Youth comprise 10 priority areas: education, employment, hunger and poverty, health, environment, drug abuse, juvenile delinquency, leisure-time activi-ties, girls and young women, and the full and effective participation of youth in society and decision-making. The World Programme of Action for Youth contains proposals for action in each of these 10 priority areas and also identifies the possible actors, including governments, non-governmental organizations (NGOs) and inter-national institutions.

In addressing the above two instruments, the present study aims to discuss the issues and actions identified in the World Programme of Action for Youth within the framework of the Jakarta Plan of

Action, with a view to enhancing the role of youth as a critical human resource of the region.

Part One of the publication reviews the progress achieved and the obstacles encountered in the formulation and implementation of youth policies and programmes during the decade since the proclamation of International Youth Year in 1985. Chapter I reviews basic facts on youth, including concepts and definitions, statistics, identification of subgroups of youth and issues for youth as identified in the World Programme of Action for Youth. Chapter II focuses on four priority areas of concern for youth in the Asian and the Pacific region, in relation to the Jakarta Plan of Action. These areas, which have been selected from the 10 priority issues identified in the World Programme of Action for Youth, are education, health, employment and the participation of youth in society. Chapter III provides an analysis of the present trends and future direction of youth policies and programmes, based on the results of a regional survey conducted by the secretariat. The analysis includes three aspects of youth policies: formulation, objectives and implementation.

Part Two of the publication reviews a series of case studies of the ongoing activities of leading youth organizations in the Asia-Pacific region in each of the four priority areas identified in this report: education, health, employment and the participation of youth in society. The purpose of this part is to showcase the many innovative approaches adopted by NGOs in the region as a basis for possible replication by other organizations.

Part Three contains the report of the Asia-Pacific Meeting on Human Resources Development for Youth (22-26 October 1996, Beijing), including the Beijing Statement on Human Resources Development for Youth in Asia and the Pacific. The Meeting was convened in pursuance of Commission resolution 52/4.

In preparing the present study, the secretariat relied, *inter alia*, on information obtained from a questionnaire survey of youth policies and programmes in the region, in pursuance of General Assembly resolution 47/85 of 16 December 1992 on policies and programmes involving youth. That resolution invited the regional commissions, together with regional and youth-serving organizations, to undertake a comprehensive review of the progress achieved and the obstacles encountered in the formulation and implementation of youth policies and programmes. The ESCAP secretariat conducted the survey in 1994 and 1995 distributing two sets of questionnaires, one on youth policies and the other on youth programmes, to governmental focal points on youth matters and to concerned NGOs. Responses were received from 29 government agencies and 33 NGOs.

The present study was originally prepared by the ESCAP secretariat as a background document for the Asia-Pacific Meeting on Human Resources Development for Youth (22-26 October 1996, Beijing). It has been subsequently revised to reflect the deliberations of that Meeting. The secretariat hopes that the publication will serve to promote regional cooperation in promoting effective youth policies and programmes in countries of the Asian and Pacific region.

The secretariat wishes to express its gratitude to the Government of China for having provided the funds to enable the secretariat to produce this publication.

# Part One:

# REVIEW OF YOUTH POLICIES AND PROGRAMMES

# Basic Facts about Youth  I

## A.  CONCEPTS AND DEFINITIONS OF YOUTH

To set the stage for the issue-oriented discussion on the youth situation in the Asian and Pacific region in the following chapters, this chapter reviews some basic concepts and facts concerning youth both in the region and globally.

Why is it important to recognize youth as a distinct group in society?  What are the concepts that underlie the term "youth"? According to a United Nations report on the global situation of youth in the 1990s, youth is perceived as:

> a transitional stage from childhood dependencies and vulnerabilities to the rights and duties of adults. ... Adolescence (15 to 17 years of age) is generally regarded as an interim period during which society ceases to regard the individual as a child, but does not yet accord the individual the full legal status and roles of adulthood.  While young adults (persons aged 18 to 24 years) are accorded the age of majority, they often do not enjoy full adult status with access to family, professional and political rights.  Before young people have the opportunity to pass through this transitional

stage, termed 'youth', they are often confronted with a variety of difficulties related to their health and social setting (families and neighbourhoods), educational careers and development".

The primary message of this statement is that it is important to recognize youth as a unique group in society due to the many aspects of vulnerability they face while passing through a major stage of their lives. This view is particularly important when the subject of youth is examined from the gender perspective.

In addition to a recognition of the vulnerability associated with the transitional nature of the identity of youth, it is equally important to recognize youth as a positive force, as a human resource with enormous potential for contributing to development. One way of confirming the importance of youth as a key target group for long-term development is to consider some of the related demographic issues. First, it must be recognized that each country has its own definition of youth. The range varies considerably. In conducting a recent regional survey, ESCAP found that some countries included people aged up to 35 years (e.g., Maldives and Singapore) or even 40 years (e.g., Malaysia) in their definition of youth. Others included new-born babies in the "youth" group (e.g., Thailand). Further, definitions of "youth" have been changing continuously in response to fluctuating political, economic and socio-cultural circumstances. In fact, the lack of a consistent definition of youth partly explains the scarcity of comparable statistics on youth.[1] However, most countries appear to include persons aged between 15 and 24 years in the youth group, which coincides with the United Nations definition of youth, thus indicating recognition of the differences between the physical, mental and personal characteristics as well as social status of youth and other social groups.[2]

---

[1] Of the 29 governmental agencies which responded to the regional survey, it was found that nine countries had a separate policy framework for children up to the ages of either 15 or 18 years.

[2] In fact, variations exist even within the United Nations system. In the Convention on the Rights of the Child, contained in General Assembly resolution 44/25 (1989), annex, a child is defined as a person aged below 18 years, since that is when he or she reaches maturity, or full legal age, in many countries.

It is important to note that the variations in the definitions of youth are not merely a matter of arbitrary choice by Governments; such variations actually have policy implications as the following examples illustrate.

## The Malaysian case

In its National Youth Policy, the age criterion is used to define youth as those between the ages of 15 and 40 years. This choice, according to the policy document, is based on the following considerations:

(a)    The definition is used by the country's primary youth body, the Malaysian Youth Council;

(b)    The group aged between 15 and 40 years is considered to have achieved a satisfactory maturity, and can realize maximum benefit from all planned programmes;

(c)    The group comprises a large percentage of the population of Malaysia (42.3 per cent or 7.6 million). Any effort to develop the group can have a large impact nationwide.

The Malaysian youth policy sees youth as potential leaders as well as participants in national planning at all levels. Hence, the policy emphasizes qualities such as responsibility, maturity and leadership among youth. The age span between 15 and 40 years responds to those requirements. Also, at the ages between 30 and 40 years, the majority of youth will have become financially and socially secure, and well-established in their careers. In fact, several have already, or will in the near future, become State ministers of Parliament or Cabinet members. Thus they will be able to contribute to, or advocate for, the youth development process, both at the local and the national levels.

## The Thai case

Youth are defined in Thailand's National Youth Promotion and Coordination Act of 1978 as persons up to the age of 25 years. The Act stipulated the establishment of a National Youth Bureau as the national-level coordinating body with the main functions of coordination, and policy and plan formulation in relation to children and youth from birth to the coming of age at 25 years in the traditional Thai context. Later, it was found that the stipulated age range created difficulty in programme implementation, as the process required different strategies and mechanisms for each age group according to child development concepts and principles. Two age groups were then identified: (a) children aged 0 to 14 years; and (b) youth aged 15 to 25 years. However, no revision of the Act has been undertaken and the legislative definition of youth still remains from 0 to 25 years.

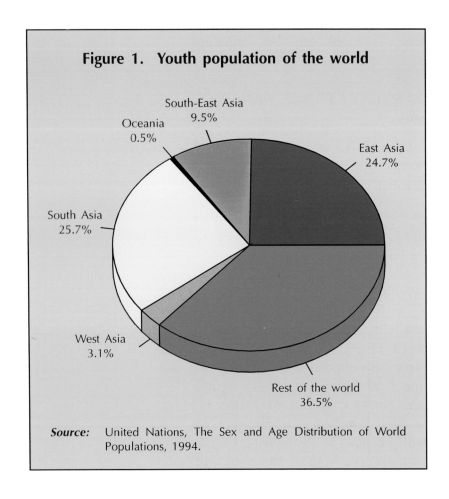

**Figure 1. Youth population of the world**

Source:   United Nations, The Sex and Age Distribution of World Populations, 1994.

The global total of young people rose from 460 million in 1950 to 1.03 billion in 1995. This figure is projected to increase to 1.3 billion by the year 2025. The majority of youth live in developing countries, where that portion of the population is estimated to have increased from 768 million (81.5 per cent) in 1985 to 864 million (84.0 per cent) in 1995, and is projected to increase further to 89 per cent by the year 2025. As of 1995, over 60 per cent of the world's youth are estimated to have been living in the developing countries of Asia and the Pacific (figure 1).

The annual growth rate of the youth population fell rapidly in most regions of the world from between 3 and 4 per cent in the late 1960s to between 1 and 2 per cent in the late 1980s. Even among the developing regions of the world, the average annual growth during the period 1985-1989 was 2 per cent, lower than the 2.8 per cent recorded in the previous five-year period. The youth population growth rate was projected to decline by 1995. East Asia in particular has seen a dramatic decline and the region experienced a negative growth rate in the youth population between 1990 and 1995 (figure 2).

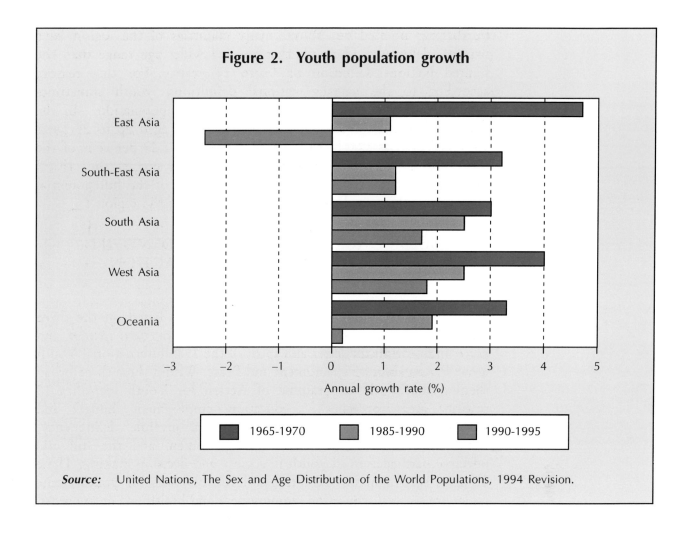

**Figure 2. Youth population growth**

Annual growth rate (%)

■ 1965-1970    ■ 1985-1990    ■ 1990-1995

*Source:* United Nations, The Sex and Age Distribution of the World Populations, 1994 Revision.

However, United Nations statistics for 1992 indicate that the youth population growth rate remained high in the South Asian subregion, standing at an estimated 2.5 per cent annually throughout the period between 1965 to 1990. The subregion also includes a few countries in which the youth population is growing at a rate of more than 3 per cent per annum, including Bangladesh (3.5 per cent) and the Islamic Republic of Iran (3.3 per cent). On average, the youth population constitutes approximately 19 per cent of the total population of the countries in the ESCAP region, higher than the total global youth population which was estimated to be 17.8 per cent (1.03 billion) in 1995. Some countries in the ESCAP region have even larger youth population ratios, including Bangladesh (21 per cent), Indonesia (21 per cent), Thailand (21 per cent) and Viet Nam (20 per cent) as of 1995. China and the Republic of Korea dropped out of the list of "above-20 per cent countries" due to a decline in their birth rates in recent years.

Further, as pointed out above, many countries of the region have national definitions of youth that cover a wider age range than the United Nations definition of 15 to 24 years. For that reason, according to the varying national definitions, youth sometimes constitute over 50 per cent of a total national population. In the case of Thailand, for example, because all those aged up to 25 years are considered as youth, that group comprises 52.29 per cent of the total Thai population. These demographic data suggest the critical importance of the development and integration of the full potential of youth in the overall development strategies of the region.

## B. ISSUES CONCERNING YOUTH AS IDENTIFIED IN THE WORLD PROGRAMME OF ACTION FOR YOUTH

The World Programme of Action for Youth is based on the three underlying themes of *distributive justice*, *popular participation* and *peace*, in line with the letter and spirit of the 1985 International Youth Year: Participation, Development and Peace. Within these three broad themes, the World Programme of Action for Youth identifies 10 priority areas for youth: education, employment, hunger and poverty, health, environment, drug abuse, juvenile delinquency, leisure-time activities, girls and young women, and the full and effective participation of youth in society and decision making. These 10 areas shed light on the different levels of issues for youth; some issues are sectoral (education, employment and health), some are cross-sectoral (hunger and poverty, environment, leisure-time activities, and the full and effective participation of youth in society and decision making), and yet others address the special subgroups of youth (drug abuse, juvenile delinquency, and girls and young women).

Therefore, the 10 priority areas identified in the World Programme of Action for Youth are neither mutually exclusive nor do they exclude the possibility of new priorities which may be identified in the future. For example, specific needs of girls and young women should be recognized in each sectoral and cross-sectoral context. Likewise, poverty is an issue that affects all of the sectoral issues. These overlaps possibly result from the dual characteristics of youth, namely, vulnerability and potential. When an issue is seen from the "protection-for-the-weak" point of view, which is often associated with the vulnerability aspect of youth, then the focus tends to be on the specific deprived subgroups. On the other hand, when an issue is considered from the point of realizing of potential human capital of youth in social, political as well as economic development, then the focus tends to be on the more general sectoral and development policies that affect broader sectors of the society, of which youth is a part. Several of the 10 priority areas identified under the World Programme of Action for Youth are discussed in chapter I in the context of the region, with orientation towards the Jakarta Plan of Action on Human Resources Development which views youth more as a potential human resource for the development of society, rather than as a group that requires protection.

## C. SUBGROUPS OF YOUTH

While the positive view of youth as prescribed in the Jakarta Plan of Action on Human Resources Development is valuable, the special needs of some of the subgroups of youth, especially those of vulnerable groups, should be duly recognized. As stated in the Guidelines for further planning and suitable follow-up in the field of youth, endorsed by General Assembly resolution 40/14 in 1985, it is more significant to focus on young people as a broad category comprising various subgroups, rather than as a single demographic entity. The Guidelines provide proposals for specific measures to address the needs of such subgroups as young people with disabilities, rural and urban youth, and young women. Among the various subgroups of youth, two deserve special attention in the context of the ESCAP region: girls and young women, and rural youth.

Girls and young women in many countries of the ESCAP region comprise one of the most vulnerable groups in society. As the World Programme of Action for Youth points out, "girls are often treated as inferior and are socialized to put themselves last, thus undermining their self-esteem. Discrimination and neglect in childhood can initiate a lifelong downward spiral of deprivation and exclusion from the social mainstream". Young women are especially likely to suffer from long-entrenched discrimination, practices and habits. On the one hand, young women receive little or no return for their huge contributions to both the economy and society. On the other hand, young women are often denied the same opportunities as men for training and paid employment, and so are prevented from maximizing their individual development and participation in society. Fundamental gender bias, which is deeply rooted in many societies of the region, negatively affects young women in particular; this has strong implications for girls and young women with regard to the accessibility of opportunities and participation in society in general. The World Programme of Action for Youth notes that "one of the most important tasks of youth policy is to improve the situation of girls and young women".

# Box 1. Feminization of poverty

Gender bias and inequities in opportunities, driven by overwhelming poverty, marginalize young girls in the developing world.

"Sabina Yasmin, a 16-year-old girl from a remote village in Bangladesh, was sexually abused by a young man who promised to marry her. Sabina was pregnant. Her mother brought her to a village abortionist who inserted a stick into Sabina's uterus to induce abortion. Infection and pain ensued. She was brought to the hospital at a great deal of expense to her family, who borrowed money with interest to pay for her medical care. Her brothers had no sympathy, her family became outcasts and Sabina unmarriageable."

Under absolute poverty, women suffer the most. Poverty has driven women in the Asian and Pacific region into low-status, low-paying occupations in domestic service or in organized prostitution, frequently as migrants away from their homes, exposing them to considerable risk of economic exploitation and sexual abuse.

Within the family, poverty strikes women harder, especially in South Asia. As women are entrusted with the responsibilities of home management, the limited resources of poor families go to boys and men under the patriarchal system. The majority of women in the region reside in rural areas or urban slums, and are engaged in subsistence agriculture or in the informal sector with little or no legislative protection and trade union support. Rapid technological advances are likely to devalue the traditional skills of women, thus jeopardizing their survival and pushing them into extreme poverty.

In spite of some increases in the participation levels of women in the workforce, significant gender inequalities persist in most countries of the region. Women often work in low-paying, unprotected and irregular types of employment. Production units in export processing and manufacturing, where workers are predominantly female, are often characterized by low wages and exploitative working conditions.

Accompanying the feminization of poverty is the violation of human rights for women. In addition to the abuse and harassment of women within the family, violence and abuse often take the form of trafficking in women, sometimes carried out across international borders. Young women from poor families are bought and sold like commodities, at times with the knowledge and tacit approval of poverty-stricken parents. These women are not only subjected to systematic physical and sexual abuse and economic exploitation, but they are also exposed to the risk of HIV/AIDS.

Against this background, the 1995 Fourth World Conference on Women at Beijing declared the following regional youth objectives for Asia and the Pacific: (a) the promotion of community-based sexual education programmes for young women with special emphasis on indigenous and migrant women; (b) the outlawing of female genital mutilation, with the support of a public awareness campaign; (c) ending prostitution and trafficking in women; (d) the reduction of the harmful effects of structural adjustment policies; (e) the implementation of measures to decrease excessive violence and the stereotyping of women in the mass media; and (f) ensuring equal educational opportunities for females at all ages.

---

*Sources:* "Youth: Partners for Action," Information sheet distributed at the Fourth World Conference on Women, Beijing, 11 September 1995.

ESCAP, 1995. "Jakarta Declaration for the Advancement of Women in Asia and the Pacific", report on the Second Asian and Pacific Ministerial Conference on Women in Development, Jakarta, 7-14 June 1994.

Kurtz, Kathleen M. and Prather, Cynthia J. Improving the Quality of Life of Girls, UNICEF, New York, 1995.

"Gender Bias: Perspectives from the Developing World," Fact Sheet compiled by Advocates for Youth, August 1995.

The majority of the youth population in the region is made up of young rural people whose roles in the development of their societies are particularly important. Simultaneously, the problems that rural youth face are often more acute than those which confront their urban counterparts because of the urban-rural gap in development which is predominant in many countries. In many ways, rural youth in the ESCAP region are one of the most disadvantaged sectors of the population as a result of the general situation found in the countryside. This situation is characterized by poverty, exploitation, lack of access to land, illiteracy, lack of stable work, isolation, unsanitary conditions and little participation in the decision making processes which affect the lives of the people themselves. In most of the developing countries of the region, the majority of young people will continue to live in rural areas for the foreseeable future.

The other aspect of the rural youth issue has to do with the massive urbanization process now occurring in many countries of the region. Rural youth are being uprooted from their families and communities because rural-urban migration is more likely to take place among youth than any other population group. The ratio of the youth population living in urban areas is steadily increasing and, according to United Nations projections, will reach 53.2 per cent by the year 2000 (compared with 44.8 per cent in 1985 and a projected 48.2 per cent in 2025 for the entire world population). The issues affecting rural youth which stem from urban migration thus warrants special attention. In many countries of the ESCAP region, rapid economic growth has created socio-cultural problems that have impacted heavily on youth from disadvantaged and low income groups. The desire to emulate the lifestyles of the urban "neo-rich" population, that have benefitted from the economic boom, has resulted in an erosion of cultural values and the uprooting of youth from their families and traditional values. Such factors have exacerbated the problems associated with urban migration of youth, including drug addiction, prostitution and HIV/AIDS.

Obviously, individual youth can belong to a number of subgroups; for example, a youth can be "female", "rural" and "disabled" at the same time. Therefore, the significance of recognizing subgroups lies in comprehending the special needs of a particular youth group, and especially those of vulnerable groups, and not with dividing youth into several categories.

# Box 2.  Urbanization and youth

Urbanization is a phenomenon of youth. Young people make urban life what it is and they bring changes to it for better or for  worse. It is in cities that young people see opportunities and new ideas. It is in cities that they see slums, traffic jams, pollution, drugs, prostitution, family breakups and loneliness.  Yet it is in cities that they find each other in a coalition for experiments towards a better future. With the rapid pace of rural-urban migration among youths in the Asian and Pacific region, and the resulting acute urban problems, there is all the more reason for youths to initiate actions for change and to lead Governments and other community members in meeting the challenges of urbanization.

Among the cases provided by Kato (1996) are the *Bangkok Forum in Thailand* and the *Youth Coalition for Human Rights in Pakistan*. The Bangkok Forum is a loose coalition of young journalists, academicians, NGO personnel and community leaders. It aims to promote public awareness of the human aspects of urban life in Bangkok, such as the conservation of neighbourhoods, the improvement of the aesthetics of city life, and the restructuring and reform of the city's bureaucracy.  It organizes events which are easy for everyone to participate in, even children.

In 1995, a forum was organized at a Muslim community facing eviction due to an expressway project. Participants were given a tour of the community and served traditional Muslim dishes, as part of an event which was planned to give them a chance to appreciate the local culture and heritage. Young journalists were involved in both the planning and reporting of the activities.

Youth Coalition for Human Rights is an NGO based in Lahore, Pakistan. It was started by students majority in different areas: philosophy, education and psychology. The group identified a large squatter area and organized community schools for children who had no opportunity to go to public schools.  The group while still pursuing their own education, contribute their time to teach at the community schools and assist to participate in various community activities.

The UN Habitat II Conference, held from 3 to 14 June 1996 in Istanbul, Turkey, emphasized the role of both the private sector and civil society in determining the physical and socio-economic landscape of cities, including youth groups. The main youth caucus at the Habitat II named itself "Youth for Habitat II".  This group organized to raise issues concerning youth in human settlements.

"Youth for Habitat II" agreed to set up an advisory board and a youth facilitators group with the following objectives: 1) to provide feedback on a youth vision statement presented at Habitat II; 2) to facilitate involvement of youth in the UN system; 3) to promote fund raising for projects; and 4) to initiate special programmes for youth.

*Sources:*     United Nations Development Programme. Urban Links. April 1996, no. 15.

Kato, Mayumi, 1996. "Municipality and Youth Partnership".  Presented at the Conference on Youth and Urban Living, Kuala  Lumpur, 9-11 April 1996.

# Issues Affecting    II
# Youth in Asia and
# the Pacific

## A. PRIORITY ISSUES UNDER THE FRAMEWORK OF THE JAKARTA PLAN OF ACTION ON HUMAN RESOURCES DEVELOPMENT

The World Programme of Action for Youth builds on the guidelines and themes identified for the International Youth Year, and also reflects other recent international instruments related to youth policies and programmes. The World Programme of Action for Youth provides suggestions for policy-making as well as programme design and delivery. It is intended to serve as a model for integrated action by all parties concerned in more effectively addressing the problems experienced by young people and enhancing their participation in society.

As detailed in chapter I, the 10 priority areas for youth identified by the World Programme of Action for Youth include different types of issues related to youth: sectoral, cross-sectoral and those issues which are related to the various subgroups. Therefore, those 10 areas may not be considered as parallel in their nature. But they do shed light on three different aspects of concern in society over youth issues: (a) the specific impact and implications of sectoral policies on youth which should be clearly recognized (sectoral issues); (b) the potential of youth which should be mobilized in order to tackle important issues of society in general (cross-sectoral issues); and (c) the needs of particularly vulnerable subgroups of youth which should always be kept in mind, in order to ensure the full integration of these subgroups into the mainstream of society (subgroups of youth).

The framework of the Jakarta Plan of Action on Human Resources Development in the ESCAP Region sheds a more focused light on the 10 priority areas. The concept of human resources development introduced in the Jakarta Plan of Action is a continuing and iterative process, comprising three interdependent components: (a) *investment* in human resources to enhance productive capabilities; (b) the *utilization* of those human resources to produce increased output; and (c) the participation of human beings in the *consumption* of the benefits arising out of that increased output through an *enhanced quality of life*. As Figure 3 shows, each of the three components of human resources development is interdependent.

Figure 3 illustrates this "HRD process in the Jakarta Plan of Action". The "utilization" link in the Figure advocates that investment in human capital in the form of health and education provides healthier and higher levels of skilled labour. Where private markets cannot solve bottleneck problems in the social infrastructure, public policies have their legitimate roles. Human infrastructure, such as literacy and numeracy, should be among the top priorities for public investment. Human capital investment policy plays two important roles: (a) securing basic

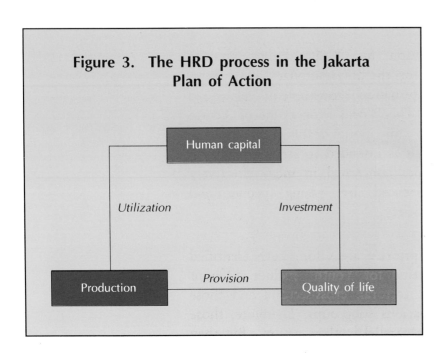

Figure 3. The HRD process in the Jakarta Plan of Action

health care and education for the poor and deprived youth (especially young females) enabling their mobilization into the labour market; and (b) providing vocational and managerial training (preferably utilizing private sector entities) to upgrade the quality of labour supply.

The first role helps to alleviate rural underemployment, while the second role helps to meet the increasing demand for middle-layer labour (e.g., factory foremen and middle managers in the hotel industry) in some high-growth Asian countries. One reservation about publicly provided education, however, would be that higher and relatively more expensive education should be carefully appraised, using benefit-cost analysis. In doing so, current and future labour demand in each category should be taken into account.

The "provision" link in the Figure indicates that, as a result of upgraded labour input into domestic production, consumers gain access to a wider variety of goods and services, leading to higher levels of household utility usage and thus to higher social welfare. In other words, they gain higher standards of living. With higher incomes from the production of high-quality goods and services, households will be able to invest more in health care and education for their children.

Four of the 10 priority areas under the World Programme of Action for Youth deserve special attention under the framework of the Jakarta Plan of Action on Human Resources Development: (a) education; (b) health; (c) employment; and (d) full and effective participation of youth in society and decision making. "Education" and "health" are broadly classified under the cycle of *investment in human resources*, while "employment" is classified under *utilization of human resources*, and "full and effective participation of youth" is covered under the *participation of human beings in sharing the benefits of development*.

Since the Jakarta Plan of Action on Human Resources Development represents a comprehensive policy framework for human resources development in the Asian and Pacific region, it was considered that one criterion for selection of priority areas for inclusion in this report should be the applicability of the issue to the three components of the above-mentioned HRD process. Of the 10 priority areas listed under the World Programme of Action for Youth, the above-mentioned four areas clearly meet this criterion.

Given that the four areas are common to both the Jakarta Plan of Action on Human Resources Development and the World Programme of Action for Youth, they thus represent priority areas for *human resources development of youth* in Asia and the Pacific.

Each of these four priority areas is discussed in this chapter, with frequent references to two subgroups of youth in particular, girls and young women, and rural youth. In the ESCAP region these two subgroups require special attention for the reasons detailed in chapter I of this review. Therefore, while chapter II does not incorporate independent sections for any particular subgroups of youth or broad cross-sectoral issues, such as hunger and poverty, special attention is given in the discussion on sectoral issues to subgroups, as well as to related cross-sectoral issues.

## B.  EDUCATION

The World Programme of Action for Youth lists three main concerns regarding the current systems of education in the world. The first is the inability of many parents in developing countries to send their children to school because of local economic and social conditions. The second concerns the paucity of educational opportunities for the more disadvantaged subgroups of youth: girls and young women, migrants, refugees, displaced persons, street children, indigenous youth minorities, young people in rural areas and young people with disabilities. The third concerns the quality of education, its relevance to gainful employment and its usefulness for assisting young people in the transition to full adulthood and active citizenship.

The Jakarta Plan of Action on Human Resources Development also emphasizes the need for strengthening education and training as the most critical process for increasing the productivity of human resources. The proposals for action contained in the Jakarta Plan of Action on Human Resources Development embody a comprehensive view of education, encompassing the formal education system at all levels as well as lifelong education in the form of adult and continuing education in non-formal settings. Training is similarly broadly conceived to include skills development through post-school vocational and technical training, on-the-job training and community-based training. Broad-based training efforts are essential to meeting today's rapidly developing technology and changing needs of society.

## Basic education

Basic education is important since the human life cycle requires that basic competencies and life skills be acquired at an early age, which largely defines the quality of life of youth. According to United Nations Educational, Scientific and Cultural Organization (UNESCO) statistics, global school enrolment expanded rapidly during the 1960s and the 1970s at an average annual rate of 3.7 per cent, followed by a slowdown in growth to 1.1 per cent during the 1980s. In the ESCAP region, all the developed and most of the higher income developing countries of Asia and the Pacific have either achieved or come close to achieving universal primary education. But for the poorer countries of the region, much requires to be done before the target can be realized. As of 1992, the gross primary enrolment ratios for Afghanistan and Pakistan were only 31 and 44 per cent respectively of all primary school-aged children; in Afghanistan, the ratio has dropped by 3 per cent since 1980. The asymmetry of the data broken down by gender for primary school enrolment is a critical issue, particularly in South Asia (see figure 4). The gross enrolment rates for girls in primary education in 1992 were 30, 43 and 27 per cent below those for boys in Afghanistan,

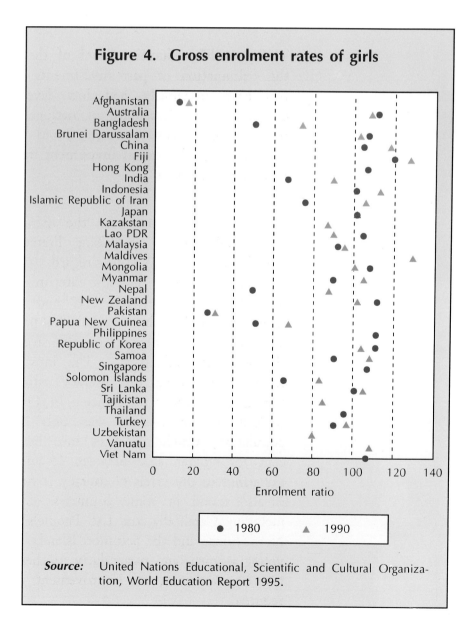

**Figure 4. Gross enrolment rates of girls**

Source: United Nations Educational, Scientific and Cultural Organization, World Education Report 1995.

21

Pakistan and Nepal, respectively, although the gap has closed by 12 per cent in Afghanistan and 15 per cent in Nepal since 1980. The gender imbalance as well as the general levels of the primary school enrolment ratios are also problems in some countries of other subregions; for example, in Papua New Guinea, the male-female primary enrolment gap stood at 13 per cent in 1992 compared with 15 per cent in 1980. In the Lao People's Democratic Republic, the gap expanded from 19 per cent in 1980 to 30 per cent in 1992.

**Literacy levels**

The prevailing education level of the adult population represents the culmination of past investments in education. In countries that have previously had low levels of investment in basic education as a percentage of national income or per child, any policy commitment to pursue rapid improvement in the overall educational level requires investment in adult education, particularly literacy programmes.

While most countries in the ESCAP region have achieved considerable success in raising literacy levels, some have made limited headway in this regard, particularly in South Asia. Although the adult literacy rate in South Asia rose from 46.6 to 50.2 per cent between 1990 and 1995, it is still significantly lower than either the average 83.6 per cent for other developing countries in the region, or the average of 73.4 per cent for all developing countries. The most urgent issue that requires attention regarding the literacy situation of the South Asian subregion is gender imbalance. In 1992, the literacy rate of adult women in South Asia was only 53 per cent of the male population, which translates into literacy rates of only 37 per cent for women aged between 15 and 24 years. In fact, gender imbalance in the levels of literacy is not limited to South Asia, but is also found in some countries of Indochina and the Pacific, including Cambodia, the Lao People's Democratic Republic, Papua New Guinea and the Solomon Islands. Given the important role of young women, and particularly mothers, as the prime educators of future generations, an improvement in the situation is urgently required.

## Table 1.  Estimated rates of adult literacy by gender, 1990-1995

| Region/Country | Both sexes | | Male | | Female | |
|---|---|---|---|---|---|---|
| | 1990 | 1995 | 1990 | 1995 | 1990 | 1995 |
| **East Asia and Oceania** | **80.3** | **83.6** | **88.2** | **90.6** | **72.2** | **76.3** |
| Brunei Darussalam | 85.1 | 88.2 | 90.5 | 92.6 | 79.0 | 83.4 |
| China | 77.8 | 81.5 | 87.0 | 89.9 | 68.1 | 72.7 |
| Fiji | 89.2 | 91.6 | 92.0 | 93.8 | 86.3 | 89.3 |
| Indonesia | 81.6 | 83.8 | 88.3 | 89.6 | 75.3 | 78.0 |
| Lao PDR | 51.5 | 56.6 | 65.1 | 69.4 | 38.6 | 44.4 |
| Malaysia | 80.2 | 83.5 | 86.9 | 89.1 | 73.6 | 78.1 |
| Mongolia | 79.9 | 82.9 | 86.6 | 88.6 | 73.2 | 77.2 |
| Myanmar | 81.3 | 83.1 | 87.8 | 88.7 | 75.0 | 77.7 |
| Papua New Guinea | 68.1 | 72.2 | 77.8 | 81.0 | 57.4 | 62.7 |
| Philippines | 93.6 | 94.6 | 94.0 | 95.0 | 93.2 | 94.3 |
| Republic of Korea | 97.1 | 98.0 | 99.0 | 99.3 | 95.2 | 96.7 |
| Singapore | 89.1 | 91.1 | 95.1 | 95.9 | 83.0 | 86.3 |
| Thailand | 93.3 | 93.8 | 95.6 | 96.0 | 91.2 | 91.6 |
| Viet Nam | 90.7 | 93.7 | 94.8 | 96.5 | 87.0 | 91.2 |
| **South Asia** | **46.6** | **50.2** | **59.8** | **62.9** | **32.6** | **36.6** |
| Afghanistan | 27.1 | 31.5 | 42.1 | 47.2 | 11.2 | 15.0 |
| Bangladesh | 35.3 | 38.1 | 46.7 | 49.4 | 23.2 | 26.1 |
| Bhutan | 37.2 | 42.2 | 51.2 | 56.2 | 23.2 | 28.1 |
| India | 48.4 | 52.0 | 62.4 | 65.5 | 33.5 | 37.7 |
| Islamic Republic of Iran | 62.4 | 68.6 | 72.3 | 77.7 | 52.1 | 59.3 |
| Maldives | 92.2 | 93.2 | 92.5 | 93.3 | 91.9 | 93.0 |
| Nepal | 24.4 | 27.5 | 37.2 | 40.9 | 11.4 | 14.0 |
| Pakistan | 34.2 | 37.8 | 46.3 | 50.0 | 20.9 | 24.4 |
| Sri Lanka | 88.7 | 90.2 | 92.6 | 93.4 | 84.8 | 87.2 |

***Sources:***   UNESCO, Division of Statistics, 1996; National Ministries of Education, 1996.

## Quality of education

The issue concerning quality of education has become increasingly important, in view of the persistent problems of drop-out and repetition. The poor quality of teaching staff, physical environment and teaching materials often discourages students from regular attendance at school and serves to increase drop-out rates. It has been widely observed in the ESCAP region that national education programmes concentrate on enrolment figures and fail to implement remedies for absenteeism, drop-outs and students repeating their grades. According to United Nations Children's Fund (UNICEF) statistics, the percentage of children reaching grade 5 in 1990 in South Asia was: Afghanistan, 13 per cent; Pakistan, 37 per cent; and Sri Lanka, 92 per cent. In order to tackle both the quantitative and the qualitative challenges of attaining universal primary education, more resources need to be geared toward primary schooling. The numeracy (ability to make numerical calculations) of the general population in particular has been suggested by many development studies as a prerequisite for economic development. In that regard, India has announced plans to quadruple spending on primary education over the five years from 1996 to 2000, while increasing the budget for higher education by 50 per cent.

The formal primary school is the principal vehicle for primary education. However, in view of the resource constraints faced by the Governments of low income countries, other complementary non-formal and flexible approaches are required in ensuring universal primary education. Two examples are community-based approaches aimed at enhancing educational understanding and support of parents and other caretakers, and "second chance" primary education for out-of-school children and youth.

Another concern related to quality is the efficiency and effectiveness of the education system in providing adequate productive manpower to meet the requirements of the rapid socio-economic and technological changes taking place in the region. Throughout the ESCAP region, and particularly in South Asia, external inefficiency is reflected in high unemployment rates among the educated. Inefficiency sometimes takes the form of "mismatch" between qualification of workers and the types of work opportunities available to them. For example, tertiary-educated workers are sometimes employed in jobs that do not require their qualifications.

Under the present rapidly changing needs of the labour market, workers have to be equipped with marketable skills that can be readily acquired. Advances in technology and communications, coupled with demand for improved productivity, present new challenges and new opportunities for employment. Young people are among the most severely affected by these developments. In that regard, close links with, and direct involvement of, the private sector in skills training have proven to be effective. Through the development of close links with the employers, the mismatch of skills in labour supply and demand could be effectively mitigated through reducing the time lag between the education and training of the potential labour force and the demand of the labour market.

# Box 3. Innovative education

The educational systems of many developing countries do not take into account the problems faced by young school leavers. Instead of promoting the potential for gainful self-employment or marketable skills, they tend to have strong motivation for wage employment, often in government establishments. Most of the educated youth in the rural areas flock to towns and cities in search of jobs, the numbers of which are never sufficient because of slow economic growth and increases in population. The disadvantaged, in particular, are unable to continue in the education system long enough to acquire sufficient knowledge and skills to match the requirements of the job market.

To tackle this problem, the UNESCO Principal Regional Office for Asia and the Pacific (PROAP) in 1989, launched the Joint Innovative Project on Education for Promoting the Enterprise Competencies of Children and Youth. The purpose of the project is to examine how primary and secondary school leavers can be adequately prepared in advance to enter the world of work, equipped with the necessary enterprising qualities either for the job market or for managing their women micro-businesses. The ultimate aim of the project is to contribute to the output of productive and useful young people who are creative, innovative, self-reliant and sensible risk-takers.

One of the experimental projects was undertaken in Indonesia from 1992 to 1996. The project focused exclusively on the poor out-of-school population in a rural area. The activities were integrated into the on-going community education programme, with two packages of learning materials, one of which was capable of raising the level of non-school populations to the primary level, and the other up to the junior secondary level. During the learning of Units 1-20 in the first package, a small amount of money (US$ 5) was provided to learners, which was sufficient to initiate a very small enterprise such as

vegetable buying and selling. During this practice, the foundation of basic entrepreneurial skills were developed in learning groups, centred on actual practical problems of real-life income generation. After Unit 20, the learners qualified for a loan, at an interest rate of 2 per cent, from a cooperative. This led to larger enterprises such as the production and trading of various types of food and prepared meals, bananas, seaweed, firewood and souvenirs. Programme facilitators, who assisted in the enterprise implementation, where drawn from different departments (industry, commerce, fisheries, cooperatives, animal husbandry), together with local professionals, village elders and local community education staff.

**Results:** The catalytic funding for the enterprises was critical but limited, and loans from commercial banks were restricted due to the lack of collateral. Obtaining the required technical knowledge and skills to improve the enterprise operations was difficult. Nonetheless the activities increased the income of the participants and motivated participation and achievement in basic education (which was a prerequisite to obtaining loans). Using the cooperative to manage and develop the funds proved effective.

**Follow-up:** Active research on training models and materials and learning materials development for enterprise education, to be conducted by seven regional learning centres (BPKBS) in collaboration with the Directorate of Technical Staff Development and Teacher Training Colleges (IKIPs); testing the models as a pilot project in seven provinces and, if successful, disseminating the models to all 27 provinces in the country and integrated them with basic and continuing education; monitoring, supervising, and formative evaluation and summation by the directorate of Community Education and the Educational Research and Development (Balitbang Dikbud) or private research institutions.

*Sources:*    UNESCO Principal Regional Office for Asia and the Pacific, 1990, Innovative Education for Promoting the Enterprise Competencies of Children and Youth, Bangkok.

UNESCO Principal Regional Office for Asia and the Pacific, 1992, Education for Nurturing Enterprising Abilities, Bangkok.

Another important aspect of quality of education, quite apart from the relevance of education in the work place, is the role of education as a means to empower young people. The purpose of education should be beyond employment generation; it should be used to promote democracy and good governance and the building of civil society. Youth education is therefore a major instrument for constructive change. Youth education is a binding factor in achieving progress in the areas of health, employment and participation. Further, education, particularly for youth, can contribute to empowerment of women through gender sensitization at various educational levels. There should be a continuous effort to review the quality of education in order to ensure that the full potential of youth can be developed.

## C.  HEALTH

Young people in many developing countries of the ESCAP region suffer from poor health as a result of social conditions, including such factors as customary attitudes, harmful traditional practices and in some cases by their own actions. As the World Programme of Action for Youth points out, poor health is often caused by the lack of a healthy environment, the absence of information, awareness and support systems which promote healthy behaviour patterns in everyday life, and inadequate health services. In observing the health issues for youth, gender perspective is also of particular importance.

### A healthy environment

In a poor health environment, the risk of infectious, parasitic and water-borne diseases, as well as diarrhoea, is often high because of the use of unpotable water and very low standards of hygiene and awareness. In South Asia, an estimated 280 million people lack access to safe water, while more than 800 million people have no access to basic sanitation. Even more important than the overall status of adequate provision of safe water and a sanitary environment, is the acuteness of the rural-urban gap in that regard. In South-East Asia and the Pacific, access to safe water and basic sanitation in rural areas is 47 per cent and 38 per cent respectively, which is only two-thirds of urban access. While 84 per cent of the people in urban areas of Papua New Guinea and China have access to safe water, only 17 per cent and 56 per cent respectively of their rural counterparts have access to similar services. Statistics on access to adequate sanitation in China and Papua New Guinea indicate an even sharper contrast, with 74 per cent and 82 per cent respectively of the urban population having such facilities, compared with only 11 per cent and 7 per cent respectively of the rural population (table 2).

### Table 2.  Basic health and sanitation status

| Country or area | % of population with access to safe water 1990-1995 | | | % of population with access to adequate sanitation 1990-1995 | | | % of population with access to health services 1990-1995 | | |
| --- | --- | --- | --- | --- | --- | --- | --- | --- | --- |
| | Total | Urban | Rural | Total | Urban | Rural | Total | Urban | Rural |
| Afghanistan | 12 | 39 | 5 | – | 13 | – | 29 | 80 | 17 |
| Bangladesh | 97 | 99 | 97 | 34 | 75 | 30 | 45 | – | – |
| Cambodia | 36 | 65 | 33 | 14 | 81 | 8 | 53 | 80 | 50 |
| China | 67 | 97 | 56 | 24 | 74 | 7 | 92 | 100 | 89 |
| India | 81 | 85 | 79 | 29 | 70 | 14 | 85 | 100 | 80 |
| Indonesia | 62 | 79 | 54 | 51 | 73 | 40 | 80 | – | – |
| Lao PDR | 45 | 57 | 43 | 27 | 97 | 14 | 67 | – | – |
| Mongolia | 80 | 100 | 58 | 74 | 100 | 47 | 95 | – | – |
| Myanmar | 38 | 36 | 39 | 36 | 39 | 35 | 60 | 100 | 47 |
| Nepal | 46 | 90 | 43 | 21 | 70 | 16 | – | – | – |
| Pakistan | 79 | 96 | 71 | 33 | 62 | 19 | 55 | 99 | 35 |
| Papua New Guinea | 28 | 84 | 17 | 22 | 82 | 11 | 96 | – | – |
| Philippines | 85 | 93 | 77 | 69 | 79 | 62 | 76 | 77 | 74 |
| Thailand | 86 | 98 | 87 | 74 | 80 | 72 | 90 | 90 | 90 |
| Viet Nam | 36 | 53 | 31 | 22 | 47 | 16 | 90 | 100 | 80 |

*Source:*  United Nations Children's Fund, 1996.

The gender implication of a healthy environment is also important. Malnourishment is still an issue in some countries of the region. In South Asia, some 300 million people do not have enough to eat. In South-East Asia and the Pacific, more than a third of the children under five are malnourished, creating a situation which has a serious impact on the health status of youth.  Girl children tend to be underfed more than boys in some countries, which leads to severe effects on the health of young women in their reproductive period.  Poor maternal health and inappropriate birth-spacing have implications, both for mothers and children. In South Asia, about 80 per cent of pregnant women suffer from anaemia, the highest rate in the world. Also, about a third of all newborn babies in that subregion are underweight. One of the main reasons for the high incidence of difficult births and anaemia in women is poor nutrition and the excessive workload women and girls are made to bear from early childhood. In fact, South Asia is the only subregion of the world where, in such countries as Bangladesh, Maldives and Nepal, the female life expectancy rate is shorter than that for males, and where there are noticeably fewer women per 100 men, defying the natural sex ratio. It should be noted, however, that the health issues of women are not limited to the South Asian subregion. The maternal mortality rate in South-East Asia and the Pacific, at 295 per 100,000 live births, is more than three times higher than that in East Asia, at 92 per 100,000 live births. Early marriages and teenage pregnancies, which have continued to flourish despite legislation to the contrary in some countries, have contributed to this problem.

## Information and support systems, particularly concerning reproductive health

Poor health is often caused by lack of information. The growing consumption of tobacco, alcohol and drugs, unwarranted risk-taking and destructive activity, resulting in unintentional injuries, are often the result of a lack of awareness.

Further, in many countries of the ESCAP region, the reproductive health needs of adolescents have been largely ignored despite the fact that many women marry during the early stage of their adolescence. Countries in which the average age of first marriage for women is below 20 years include Bangladesh (16.7 years), Afghanistan (17.8 years), Nepal (17.9 years), India (18.7 years), the Islamic Republic of Iran (19.7 years) and Pakistan (19.8 years). In fact, 44 per cent of the young women in the South Asian subregion will be married before reaching the age of 19. Yet, at present, there is a lack of information and services for helping adolescents to understand their sexuality, including sexual and reproductive health, and for protecting them from unwanted pregnancies, sexually transmitted diseases including the human immunodeficiency virus/acquired immunity deficiency syndrome (HIV/AIDS).

## Box 4.  AIDS awareness programmes

In many countries in the developing world, up to two-thirds of all new HIV infections may now be occurring among youths aged between 15 and 24 years. The death toll from AIDS is expected to exceed 8 million by the year 2000, with the majority of those fatalities occurring in developing countries. Children are bearing a huge and growing burden resulting from the HIV/AIDS pandemic, either directly as sufferers or as a result of having parents, siblings and other relatives die. Many AIDS orphans lack love and family support and they risk becoming street children with all the attendant perils to health and emotional well-being. The growing number of HIV-infected mothers is expected to push up national child mortality rates. In Thailand, for example, the child mortality rate is expected to grow almost fivefold by the year 2000, because of HIV infection from maternal victims.

In 1994, in South and South-East Asia, HIV infections were estimated at 2.5 million (a million more than in 1993). In parts of northern Thailand, for example, 20 per cent of 21-year-old military recruits and 8 per cent of women attending antenatal clinics have been diagnosed as infected, yet HIV was virtually unknown in that country in 1987. In India infection rates have tripled since 1992. In fact, the HIV infection rate in Asia went from 12 per cent of the world total in 1993 to 16 per cent in 1994.

In terms of prevention, Thailand has demonstrated that condoms make a difference, as sexual transmitted diseases (STDs) nationwide fell by 77 per cent between 1986 and 1993. WHO has placed high priority on AIDS prevention in South-East Asia where national AIDS committees have been established, education and information programmes started for health workers and the general population, and laboratory facilities strengthened for screening blood for HIV.

*Sources:*   WHO; World Health Report 1995.

International Council on Management of Population Programmes, 1995; Report of the Workshop on Innovative Approaches in Youth Reproductive Health Programmes.

According to UNDP, more than two million people have been infected with HIV in the East and South-East Asian subregions. According to the World Health Organization (WHO), the HIV epidemic is spreading at a rate of over 6,000 new infections per day in the world and in many countries, 60 per cent of the new infections are found among young people aged between 15 and 24. Young women are twice as  likely to be on this list as compared with men.  The group that is most vulnerable in terms of absolute numbers comprises of single-partner married women who are exposed to infection by sexually promiscuous husbands.  Also among the most affected by the HIV/AIDS crisis, and at the receiving end of many sexually transmitted diseases, are prostitutes who often lack adequate health protection.  In addition, the incidence of unwanted pregnancies is still very high in the region, suggesting among other factors, the inadequate access of women to education about reproductive choices and to family planning services, or the lack of control over their reproductive roles in an unequal sexual partnership.

# Box 5.  Reproductive health

Increasing attention is being paid to the health of adolescents in recognition of the impact of a rapidly changing world on their behaviour and the importance of that period of life in setting the patterns which will have lifelong implications for them.

Two recent conferences, the International Conference on Population and Development and the Fourth World Conference on Women, accorded the highest priority to promoting gender equality, women's empowerment and the elimination of all forms of discrimination against women. Also, the Beijing Platform for Action firmly established that "the human rights of women and the girl child are an inalienable, integral and indivisible part of all human rights and fundamental freedom". It calls on men to share family responsibilities and to take responsibility for their reproductive and sexual behaviour.

The road to women's empowerment starts with reproductive health. The task of the United Nations Population Fund (UNFPA) is to ensure that: (a) a life cycle approach is taken with respect to women's health; (b) women have the information and services they need for bearing and bringing up their children in health and safety; and (c) women have control over, and decide on matters related to their sexuality, including sexual and reproductive health, free from coercion, discrimination and violence. In that context, population and development programmes, including reproductive health programmes, should be designed to serve the needs of both males and females including adolescents, and should involve women in the leadership, planning, decision making, management, implementation and monitoring processes of such programmes.

In most of the Asian countries, there have been small-scale innovative activities in youth reproductive health programmes. Jaito Tarun Sangha (National Youth Organization) in Bangladesh, which is run by young volunteers, provides primary health care to about 1,000 village and urban communities.  In India, the National Committee of Youth Organizations, which is the coordinating body of more than 60 national youth organizations, operates four regional youth training centres which include adolescent fertility as a part of their training. In

Indonesia, the youth wing of the ruling party plays a very important role in mobilizing youth, particularly young married couples. In Sri Lanka, the National Youth Service Council has been active in sex education programmes for young people.

### China:  Millions of unpaid volunteers provide ackbone of family and child care services

China, Family Planning Associations (FPAs) rely heavily on the services of unpaid volunteers, numbered in tens of millions, who generally do not provide contraceptive services (this service is undertaken by the Government) but who work in their own communities giving advice on family planning, child care and related family matters. Their main aims are to reduce the incidence of abortion due to contraceptive failure, by ensuring that couples understand the proper use of contraceptives and by campaigning for a wider choice of methods, and to educate families on the value of girl children. In Fujian Province in southern China, the FPA of Minhou County, through supervising its members' network, has been monitoring the performance of government personnel at all levels to eliminate any possible abuse. It has urged the authorities to ensure that incentives are given in the form of preferential assistance to family planning acceptors. The county government has provided special maternal and child health services to over 50,000 women of reproductive age and all their children up to the age of eight, and it has set up insurance schemes for one-daughter families, such as child safety and family planning pension insurance.

### India:  Young Inspirers make sexual and reproductive health a youth affair

Since 1993, a carefully selected group of trained male and female students aged 16 to 22 years in Lucknow, India, have been reaching fellow youths with correct information on youth sexuality and reproductive health. Calling themselves the Young Inspirers, they fully manage the project with guidance from the Family Planning Association of India. The group's three activities are:

*(Continued)*

**Box 5.** *(continued)*

(a)   In-school poster competitions, essay writing, role playing etc.;

(b)   Outreach work with employed youths, such as rickshaw pullers, mini-taxi drivers and train station workers, through lectures that heavily rely on visual aids;

(c)   Peer counselling. Group members counsel their peers at school and in residential neighbourhoods. If follow-ups are necessary, youths are referred to the counsellor at the Family Planning Association clinic.

Being youths themselves, the Young Inspirers understand the diversity of youth problems. This has led to the encouragement of youth participation in project implementation. The group's activities have thus enabled youths to express their concerns and suggest ways of overcoming their problems.

*Sources:*   Statement of the United Nations Population Fund Executive Director on the occasion of International Women's Day, 8 March 1996; United Nations Information Service/ESCAP press release, 6 March 1996.

WHO, The World Health Report 1995.

International Planned Parenthood Federation; Planned Parenthood 1996/1, "Challenges: Advocacy for reproductive health".

International Council on Management of Population Programmes; Report of the Workshop on Innovative Approaches in Youth Reproductive Health Programmes, 1995.

times starved or tortured if they fail to comply with customers' demands, some girls are broken to the point where they can never regain self-respect and dignity. This group of young people are difficult to reach with health services. They view health professionals as unfriendly, threatening and unhelpful and when they seek medical care they are reluctant to be candid. Therefore treatment does not address their needs.

## Health services

While many countries of the region have made significant advances in the provision of health care services, marked inadequacies remain. Many countries continue to suffer from inadequate medical services, with distribution heavily skewed in favour of urban areas. In Pakistan, 99 per cent of the urban population has access to health services, compared with 35 per cent of the rural population. In Myanmar, the ratio is 100 per cent and 47 per cent for the urban and rural population.

It should also be noted that access to health services is generally skewed in favour of men; consequently, poor rural women are the most neglected of all groups. General and maternal health care and the treatment of complications resulting from pregnancy and childbirth-related problems are still highly inadequate in many countries. Facilities for the treatment of infections, toxaemia and haemorrhage, which are the major causes of maternal mortality, are generally inadequate in many countries.

## D. EMPLOYMENT

### Youth unemployment

Youth unemployment and under-employment are global problems. They are part of the larger struggle to create employment opportunities for all citizens. However, there are several reasons for the higher unemployment levels among youth compared with other age groups. Unemployment in the ESCAP region is primarily found among youth, with estimates placing youth unemployment on average four times higher than non-youth unemployment (figure 5). Considerable concern has been expressed

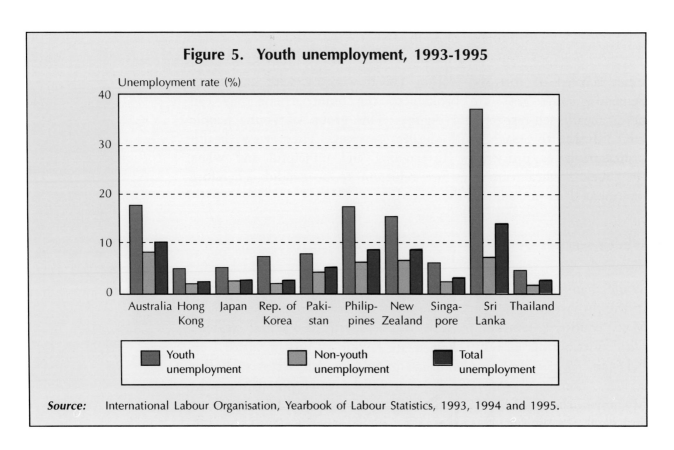

Figure 5. Youth unemployment, 1993-1995

*Source:* International Labour Organisation, Yearbook of Labour Statistics, 1993, 1994 and 1995.

in recent years about the rising level of unemployment among the educated. Among youth, unemployment affects both the educated and the uneducated, suggesting that the problem is a genuine shortage of employment opportunities.

Among the factors that could be specifically attributable causes of youth unemployment, in addition to those factors that create general unemployment, are:

(a)     Mismatching between the education and skill levels of young entrants to the labour market and the requirements of employers. In a number of developing countries, one problem is the high drop-out rate from primary and secondary education, which leads to an unskilled workforce that does not meet the requirements of prevailing technology. Another problem is the "over education" of youth in the social sciences and the scarcity in technical training opportunities, or poor links between such technical training and labour-market needs;

(b)     Relatively high minimum wage levels, particularly in developed countries and in the Pacific subregion, which discourages employers from hiring young new labour market entrants;

(c)     Discrimination against youth in recruitment, where employers value experience, proven skills and seniority.

The crisis of youth unemployment is also a crisis of opportunities for young people to independently acquire the minimum means for accommodation and housing necessary for setting up families and for participating in society. The early age of marriage prevailing in many countries of the region, where nearly 80 per cent of women and 40 per cent of men in South Asia, and some 50 per cent of women and 30 per cent of men in South-East Asia are married by the age of 24, has potentially serious economic implications with regard to youth unemployment in such households.

Further, unemployment creates a wide range of social ills that have damaging effects on young people, including the lack of skill development, low self-esteem, marginalization, impoverishment and the wasting of an enormous human resource. Such problems have become particularly serious in urban unemployment in many developing countries of the ESCAP region, because urban unemployment victimizes rural youth migrants first and brings added insecurity, rootlessness and frustration to this vulnerable subgroup. Young people who are less educated and less skilled than their urban counterparts are uprooted from the traditional system of support; consequently, they are exposed to the lowest ranks of the industrial hierarchy and have little say in matters affecting their working life. In fact, they make up the subgroup that has become the most adversely affected by mechanization and automation.

## Box 6. Rural-urban migration

The patterns of economic development whereby opportunities are concentrated in urban areas are drawing large numbers of young people out of the rural areas. But in many developing countries, the slow pace of employment generation and the adoption of labour-saving technologies in the urban sector increase the difficulties which result from the rapid pace of labour migration to urban areas.

The continued inflow to the cities of rural migrants in the expectation of employment opportunities is causing a variety of urban problems. In Kathmandu, Nepal, for example, the proliferation of slums is rapid, public transport is overcrowded and over-used, and the water supply system is not always safe. Less than 50 per cent of the population living in Nepal's urban areas have drainage, solid waste disposal and sanitation facilities. It is estimated that there are about 39 squatter settlements in Kathmandu; almost 67 per cent of the squatters are reported to be inhabited by migrants from rural areas.

In Thailand, the majority of rural-urban migrants are females. The country's migration patterns contribute to an urban population concentration of young adults and a significant gender imbalance in the urban and rural areas.

Although rural-urban migration can provide benefits for women, such as economic independence through wage income, thus delaying marriage and lowering fertility, decent employment opportunities for migrant females appear to be restricted. While large numbers of migrant women are employed in the manufacturing sector, that situation is primarily confined to young females. The older ages are more likely to be found in low-paying service sector jobs.

In general, it is the more educated who are most likely to migrate. The young and ambitious segments of the population, who have limited opportunities to use their education in rural areas, are likely to migrate to urban areas. The dilemma is how to make improvements in the level of human resources of the rural population while channeling those human resources for improvements in rural areas.

*Source:* Trends, patterns and implications of rural-urban migration in India, Nepal and Thailand. Asian Population Studies Series, no. 138; ESCAP, 1995.

## Youth in the growing labour force

The size of the labour force is expanding in most developing countries of the region. Only in a few ESCAP countries, most notably China, Singapore and Thailand, will the size of the youth labour force decrease over the next two decades. For the rest of the region, it is expected to increase from an average of 2.1 per cent per annum in the period 1955-1985 to 2.3 per cent per annum between 1985 and 2015. The number of youth entering the labour force will increase sharply in countries with high fertility, such as Bangladesh, Pakistan and the Philippines. While the opposite will occur in some countries, such as the Republic of Korea, Singapore and Thailand, based on existing trends the region's overall labour force is projected to approximately double over the next 30 years.

---

## Box 7. Vocational training: Singapore and the Republic of Korea

**Singapore**

The Institute of Technical Education (ITE) of Singapore was established in 1992 as a post-secondary technical institution targeting school leavers and working adults. ITE offers two innovative programmes:

(a) Integrated and comprehensive continuing education and training (CET) offers working adults, from 20 to 40 years of age, opportunities to enrol in academic courses from primary to pre-university levels and specific skills training programmes. In order to accommodate working adults who may face disruptions due to other commitments, the courses are conducted in self-contained modules of six-month duration;

(b) The certified on-the-job centre system (COJTC), which reaches out to workers who need to continuously upgrade their skills in order to remain relevant in their jobs. Under the COJTC system, companies with the commitment and proper training infrastructure are authorized to implement on-the-job training programmes. To date, 201 companies have been certified to undertake 2,400 programmes. ITE works for 25 per cent of the annual 10,000 school leavers,

while CET programmes provide another 60,000 education and training places annually to working adults.

**Republic of Korea**

In the Republic of Korea, the Korea Manpower Agency was established in 1982. It operates vocational training courses, national qualification testing of technical personnel and other skills-upgrading research and development programmes. The focus of work of the agency has been training and employment promotion for youth. Since 1990, the agency has been promoting employment by matching graduates of training courses and applicants for the National Technical Qualification Tests with the requirements of employers. In 1995, the agency launched the Unemployment Insurance System in 1995 for integration into an expanded employment service network system. Between 1982 and 1995, a total of 4,028 master craftsmen and over 180,000 general craftsmen were trained through the agency; the success rate in job placement is almost over 90 per cent. Nearly 3 million people have passed the National Technical Qualification Tests at various levels, which serve as a motivational tool in encouraging students to upgrade their skills as well as providing formal recognition of technical proficiency.

---

*Source:* Derived from applications for the 1995 ESCAP HRD Award, HRD Section, ESCAP.

This has strong implications for the youth labour market situation. According to International Labour Organization (ILO) estimates, more than 100 million new jobs will have to be created in the world within the next 20 years in order to provide suitable employment for the growing number of young people in the economically active populations of the developing countries. Among other subgroups, the situation of girls and young women, as well as of young people with disabilities, refugee youth, displaced persons, street children, indigenous and migrant youth, and minorities, warrants urgent attention. The problem of employment has worsened in recent years because of the global recession, which has affected developing countries the most. The disturbing fact is that economic growth is not always accompanied by expansion in employment opportunities. In that regard, the Jakarta Plan of Action on Human Resources Development advocates policies on labour-utilizing investment, including those policies which support informal sector activities and small-scale and cottage industries, pointing out the importance of

## Box 8. The Barefoot College, India, Winner of the 1995 ESCAP HRD Award

The winner of the 1995 ESCAP HRD Award was the Social Work and Research Centre of Tilonia, Rajasthan, India, better known as the "Barefoot College."

The Barefoot College was selected as the winner of the Award by an international jury of distinguished experts in the field of human resources development. In reaching its decision, the Jury was particularly impressed by the College's innovative programmes to promote employment for youth, which was the special theme for the 1995 round of the Award.

The Barefoot College is a non-formal training institute where young men and women are given practical skills by their peers. The subject and coverage of its educational programmes are determined by the villagers. The teachers in the college are local villagers. Teaching and learning are based on the practical needs of the villagers.

Remarkable achievements have been recorded by the Barefoot College. Two generations of teachers, doctors and engineers have passed through the College and are now providing basic services to support their communities. Once considered

"unemployable", these graduates have become productive members of their communities.

Rural youth have been trained and employed to run schools for boys and girls; training camps and workshops have been organized to upgrade the skills of young artisans. Trained as engineers and mechanics, the youth are providing such services as installing and maintaining solar electricity systems to provide basic lighting, and installing hand pumps to provide safe drinking water to over 1.8 million villagers.

Since 1972, some 1,300 hand pumps in the area surrounding the village were constructed and are being maintained by rural youth, all graduates of the College. There are also some 80 night schools providing literacy skills which benefit from a solar electrification system installed by the graduates.

Through conferring the 1995 ESCAP HRD Award on the Barefoot College, it is hoped that the College's innovative work will serve as a source of inspiration for further efforts to promote productive employment among youth in India, as well as other countries in the ESCAP region.

promoting self-employment and entrepreneurship. In addition to the provision of suitable education and skills training to meet the needs of the labour market, it is necessary to emphasize a labour utilization policy based on the current labour situation of the region.

## E.  EFFECTIVE PARTICIPATION

As the World Programme of Action for Youth states, the progress of society depends, to a considerable extent, on its capacity to incorporate the contribution and responsibility of youth in the building and designing of its future. In addition to mobilizing the capacity of youth for supporting today's development policies, their unique perspectives of the immediate future need to be taken into account in the formulation of long-term policies.

The economic, social and political participation of youth largely conditions the effectiveness of actions proposed in the World Programme of Action for Youth. As the Jakarta Plan of Action on Human Resources Development advocates, both the means and the results of development should be people-centred, and young people should be given an appropriate position in society to allow them to express their views on the improvement of the social, economic and cultural aspects of society. Policies should be geared toward creating an atmosphere among young people that provides possibilities for bringing about improvements in their own lives and for the future of society as a whole.

In order to fully develop the aspirations of youth for people-centred development of society, policy makers need to first understand the problems and needs of youth. Policy and programme formulation need to start with appropriate decision-taking by youth at all levels, including communities, schools and universities at the provincial and national levels, through such means as voting and the provision of appropriate status to youth organizations and leaders.

The World Programme of Action for Youth stresses that youth organizations are an important vehicle for development of participation by youth in leadership, promotion of tolerance, and increasing cooperation and exchanges between youth organizations.

## Table 3.  Statistics:  Age of legal rights and obligations

| Country or area | Age to have the right to vote law | Age to marry without consent of parents | Age to be held liable for transgression of |
|---|---|---|---|
| Azerbaijan | 18 | 18 | 14 |
| Bangladesh | 18 | 21 (m) 18 (f) | 21 (m) 18 (f) |
| Cambodia | 18 | 25 | 18 |
| China | 18 | 22 (m) 20 (f) | 16 |
| Fiji | 21 | 18 | 17 |
| Guam | 18 | 18 | 18 |
| Hong Kong | 18 | 18 | 17 |
| Indonesia | 17 | 21 | 18 |
| Islamic Republic of Iran | 15 | 15[1] | 15 |
| Japan | 20 | 20 | 20 |
| Kazakstan | 20 | 18 | 14 |
| Macau | 18 | 18 | n.a. |
| Malaysia | 21 | 16 | 16 |
| Maldives | 21 | 16 | 16 |
| Marshall Islands | 18 | 18 | 18 |
| Mongolia | 18 | 18 | 16 |
| New Caledonia | 18 | 18 | 18 |
| Niue | 18 | 21 (m) 18 (f) | 14 |
| Palau | 18 | 18 | 18 |
| Philippines | 18 | 26[2] | 29[3] |
| Republic of Korea | 20 | 18 (m) 16 (f) | 14 |
| Samoa | 21 | n.a. | n.a. |
| Singapore | 21 | 21 | 16 |
| Sri Lanka | 18 | 18 | 18 |
| Thailand | 20 | 20 | 20 |
| Turkmenistan | 18 | 18 | 18[4] |
| Tuvalu | 18 | 21 | 20 |
| Vanuatu | 18 | 22 (m) 24 (f) | n.a. |

**Source:**   ESCAP youth questionnaire, 1996.

**Notes:**   (m)  =  males.
  (f)  =  females.
 n.a.  =  not available.
  [1]  For virgins, parental consent is necessary regardless of age.
  [2]  Youth between ages 21 and 25 are obliged to ask their parents for advice on the intended marriage.
  [3]  Until the offender reaches 21, he or she will be put to the custody of the Department of Social Welfare or an authorized training and rehabilitation institution.
  [4]  Age of 14 for serious crimes.

Youth organizations can provide an effective means and opportunities for youth to participate in the mainstream of society. Youth organizations that are closely linked with the communities can bring about the melding of distinctly different issues and concerns of rural and urban youth.  While a number of

Governments in the region involve youth organizations in the formulation and implementation of youth policies, existing collaborative structures between the government and non-government sectors need to be reexamined and improved.

Bias exists among many adults that young people are the cause of social problems, not the solution; they believe that providing youth with information and knowledge poses a threat to social stability. But the promotion of the health and education of adolescents actually offers tremendous benefits for the  public good while also helping youth to fulfil their own potential.  The nature of the relationship between adults and adolescents is at the heart of the matter.  A positive outlook by an adult is more likely to elicit a positive reaction in an adolescent.  For this to happen, there are at least two prerequisites; the basic needs of young people must be met and the opportunity to use their capacities must be provided.

The following areas require improvement on the part of the Governments: formulation of a curriculum of formal education that incorporates survival skills in the context of current socio-economic realities; recognition and appreciation of youth initiative; greater access to information; education and skills training for youth empowerment; and the granting of greater priority to youth programmes.

NGOs are an important channel for youth participation in development.  Many NGOs are in regular contact with young people and thus are in a better position to mobilize them for constructive activities at the local and national levels.  They are often run by extremely dedicated and experienced youth leaders. What the NGOs need is a wider range of opportunities and recognition by the general public so that the vast resource of energy which youth represents can be put to its best use for society.  This can only be done by political will, mutual trust between Governments and NGOs, and networking of youth organizations at the local and national levels.  A Youth Ministry or its equivalent in each country could take much of the responsibility in facilitating and preparing such infrastructure for youth NGOs. Networking, in particular, helps to mobilize NGOs in different fields and with different goals in identifying and tackling common social problems such as drug abuse and HIV/AIDS.

An effective approach to networking should be bottom-up, not top-down, because needs and ideas of development reside with grassroots experiences. It is at the district level downwards that the beneficiary groups of development are located and it is towards them that programmes should be aimed. To strengthen youth NGOs, the Governments should facilitate their free and uninhibited functioning, feeding their trial-and-error results into the formation of broad national goals. Although some Governments have schemes for giving grants-in-aid to NGOs, an even greater share should go to those working with young people, especially young women. Those NGOs should also be provided with technical support and training facilities for their personnel. Governments could also set up a liaison body among NGOs and between the government and NGOs.

At the micro-level, particularly regarding the participation of rural youth in development, it is essential that a network of small-sized and often non-registered youth clubs (which may be based on agricultural cooperatives, political parties, local chambers of commerce or even Internet circles) be created so that rural youth can be associated with the delivery of the development programme benefits. The youth clubs could act as watch-dogs for the implementation of national and district-level programmes. Ideally, all three participating groups (Governments, NGOs and youth organizations), have complementary roles and responsibilities in providing an infrastructure for youth participation in development.

# Overview of National Youth Policies

III

A major portion of the questionnaire survey undertaken by ESCAP, in pursuance of General Assembly resolution 47/85, focused on the current status of youth policies and their implementation among the countries and areas of the region.[1] This chapter analyzes the results of the survey providing trends on existing youth policies and their formulation and implementation, as well as suggested areas for future strengthening.

This chapter consists of three sections. The section on *youth policy formulation* discusses the rationale behind national efforts to formulate youth policies and promote their integration into the overall development process of the country. The section on *policy*

---

[1] The secretariat received answers to the questionnaire from the following members and associate members: Azerbaijan, Bangladesh, Cambodia, China, Fiji, Guam, Hong Kong, Indonesia, Islamic Republic of Iran, Japan, Kazakstan, Kyrgyzstan, Macau, Malaysia, Maldives, Marshall Islands, Mongolia, New Caledonia, Niue, Palau, Philippines, Republic of Korea, Samoa, Singapore, Sri Lanka, Thailand, Tonga, Turkmenistan, Tuvalu and Vanuatu.

*objectives* analyses the objectives and principles of youth policies in the region and identifies selected elements that require government attention in order to further strengthen existing youth policies. Finally, the section on *policy implementation* analyses the major difficulties encountered by governments in their implementation of youth policies. It discusses the institutional issues inherent in the implementation of youth policies, analyses the characteristics of existing national youth focal point agencies, and identifies institutional factors that influence the translation of policy into programmes. It also analyses the major difficulties encountered by governments in their implementation of youth policies.

## A. POLICY FORMULATION

### Formulation

Youth and youth-related issues have continued to form part of the agenda of the United Nations. Concern over the situation of youth led the United Nations to declare 1985 as International Youth Year: Participation, Development and Peace. The International Youth Year sought to enhance awareness of the needs and aspirations of youth and to make youth activities and participation an integral part of social and economic development. A highlight of that year was the endorsement by the United Nations General Assembly of the Guidelines for Further Planning and Suitable Follow-up in the Field of Youth.

One of the main recommendations in the Guidelines was for Member States to formulate national youth policies and programmes to improve the situation of youth, and to establish coordinating structures to implement those policies and programmes. Over 100 countries and areas set up national youth coordinating committees for International Youth Year and a great part of the renewed action in the 1990s can be traced to such bodies. Unfortunately, these committees have generally faded away. Nonetheless, it is important to note that the International Youth Year provided the opportunity to realize the need and importance of coordinated efforts towards the development of youth policies and programmes. The recent survey on youth policies and programmes also confirmed that many countries in the region initiated national youth policies as a result of the observance of International Youth Year.

Why do countries need youth policies? The World Programme of Action for Youth identifies some of the reasons why a specific policy for youth is necessary:

> Young people in all countries are both a major human resource for development and key agents for social change, economic development and technological innovation. Their imagination, ideals, considerable energies and vision are essential for the continuing development of the societies in which they live. The problems that young people face as well as their vision and aspirations are an essential component of the challenges and prospects of today's societies and future generations. Thus, there is special need for new impetus to be given to the design and implementation of youth policies and programmes at all levels. The ways in which the challenges and potentials of young people are addressed by policy will influence current social and economic conditions and the well-being and livelihood of future generations.

While countries may have different incentives for adopting a youth policy, such policies need to contain a plan of action with a vision for developing youth. The motives of any country for adopting a youth policy may be based on the increasing numerical importance of the youth population, a trend which has been already reviewed, and on the growing and vigorous self-assertiveness of young people. Young people who have received formal education have acquired capacities of articulating their desire for participation in political and social life. Yet another reason may be the discontent and resentment of young people who are facing unemployment and underemployment. Many Governments, concerned with the situation of youth, traditionally undertook programmes and measures, but not as part of an explicit and comprehensive youth policy. Typically, youth policies consisted of a combination of various policies under the purview of different ministries or government departments, such as education, training, health, social affairs, employment, rural development, youth and sports, justice and defence. That type of sectoral approach, by viewing youth as clients of separate services, precludes access to those services by disadvantaged sections of youth, including slum dwellers and rural youths. As stated in a recommendation of the Regional Policy Consultation of the Commonwealth Youth Programme (Chandigarh, India, 1992), "the enunciation of youth policy is a manifestation of political will and commitment of the nation to the cause of all-round development of youth and their integration with other sections of the society".

According to the results of the ESCAP survey and information obtained from other sources, only a few countries and areas in the region had some form of youth policy prior to 1985: Bangladesh, Guam, Sri Lanka and Thailand. A few other countries, including Malaysia and India, formulated their youth policy between the period 1985 and 1990. The majority of the existing youth policies in the region were formulated following the International Youth Year (1985), and in many cases not until the 1990s, including

## Box 9. Youth policy development in Cambodia

In any country, youth represent the future. This is especially true for Cambodia, where the young constitute a sizable section of the population as a result of more than two decades of armed conflict. The development of Cambodia depends largely on harnessing and nurturing the potential of its young population. There is a definite need to evolve an overall youth policy framework that will capture the concerns of the country's young people, their visions of the future and their roles in the context of national development. Establishing a youth policy framework would provide the basic platform for developing appropriate programmes and activities for Cambodia's youth.

At the request of the Minister of Education, Youth and Sport, an ESCAP Advisory Mission visited Cambodia in March 1996 to provide assistance in the initial stages of developing a national youth policy. Through consultations with youth representatives and with concerned government officials, the Mission identified seven major issues that Cambodian youth policy should focus on: peace, order and security; education; poverty alleviation and employment; health and sanitation; environment; sports; and empowerment, participation and institutional development.

For a national youth policy to be effective, a clear understanding of the problems and needs of youth has to come first. Hence, a major part of the Mission's work was devoted to direct consultation with Cambodian youth, through two Situation Analysis Workshops (SAWs) which were held in Phnom Penh and Kampot province.

The participants in the situation analysis workshop consisted of high school and university students, disabled youth, Youth Department officials, representatives of NGOs and youth organization, school teachers and unemployed youth.

Contrary to the general belief that young people do not have a broad perspective of economic and social issues, the participants at both Workshops appeared to have a clear understanding of the general situation of their country, as well as the core issues affecting them. Some of the issues, such as peace and security (including land mines), unemployment, school-related issues and corruption in society, were listed among the priority problems at both Workshops.

Although limited in terms of the sample size, the experience of the Mission in conducting the Cambodian SAWs presents a strong case for similar workshops to be organized by government officials to obtain reliable information on the needs of Cambodian youth. The SAWs may also be utilized as opportunities for building youth groups at the grassroots level. It is possible to start this activity by taking up a few self-help projects from the suggestions made at the Workshops such as, for example, by including an exercise for project formulation and planning. In this way, the function of SAWs may be even further extended to open up new opportunities for longer-term action for youth. With that in mind, the HRD Section of ESCAP plans to continue the provision of similar services in other countries of the region.

Azerbaijan, China, Fiji, Indonesia, Hong Kong, the Islamic Republic of Iran, Kazakstan, the Philippines, Turkmenistan and Vanuatu. In China, the Government recently enacted legislation which ensures the rights of young people and which focuses on education and the participation of young people in decision-making processes. Yet some other countries were still at the early stages of planning or formulating youth policies when the survey was conducted, including Cambodia, the Marshall Islands and Mongolia.

From the above, it may be concluded that youth policy formulation is still a very recent event in the history of most countries and areas in the region, regardless of the subregion. The observance of International Youth Year certainly helped trigger country-level initiatives, but in many cases the actual formulation exercise occurred in the 1990s. Therefore, most countries and areas of the region, regardless of the individual level of national economic development, have had little experience in implementing their newly formulated youth policies. To promote the formulation of youth policies in those countries of the region which have yet to undertake such an exercise, as well as to facilitate effective implementation of policies that are already in place, it is all the more important to initiate an active regional exchange of experience.

## Integration

In addition to the formulation of a national youth policy as independent legislation, it is necessary for countries to integrate such policy into the overall development picture. A policy for youth needs to be related to, and coordinated with, other national and social policies; at the same time, a youth policy should be integrated into the overall strategy for development. It is essential that the particular needs and problems of youth be considered as an integral part of the national planning and policy-making process. A major step towards integration is to ensure that youth policy is not isolated from the other objectives of the national development plan, and that it is incorporated into the documents of the national development plan. A national youth policy should not be treated as a separate plan for young people. It should act across sectoral lines so that the needs of youth and the implications of policies on youth are duly recognized in each of the sectoral development plans. Without the mainstreaming of national youth policy, backed by an appropriate budget allocation and infra-structure for implementation, policy formulation becomes perhaps a futile exercise.

Only a limited number of countries in the region appear to have established systems for incorporating youth policies into their national development plans. For example, the Republic of Korea incorporated, for the first time, a Youth Fostering Five-Year Plan in its national development five-year plan for 1992-1996. The Philippines, too, has reflected its National Youth Development Plan of 1994 in its medium-term development plan under the section covering the human resources development strategy of youth. It stresses achievement of youth empowerment and increasing investments in youth human resources through education, training, and improved basic services in health and nutrition. Other countries that have incorporated their youth policies in their national development plans are: Azerbaijan, China, Fiji, Maldives, Malaysia, Mongolia, Singapore and Thailand. A few other countries indicated that youth policies were being considered as a part of the overall development objective, although the explicit incorporation of such legislation had yet to take place. For example, in the case of Bangladesh, human resources development is a major objective shared both in its fourth five-year plan and its youth policy.

## Box 10. Thai Business Initiative for Rural Development

Despite the impressive economic growth of Thailand, poverty persists in the rural areas, particularly in the arid north-eastern region, known as Isan. In the last few years, a new and promising HRD approach to tackling rural poverty has been pioneered by the Population and Community Development Association (PDA), an NGO based in Thailand. Called the Thai Business Initiative for Rural Development (TBIRD), the programme recruits private sector companies to sponsor HRD activities in rural areas. The founder and Chairman of PDA, Mr. Mechai Viravaidya, reasoned that not only could private companies use their entrepreneurial experience to help villagers identify business opportunities, they could also help villagers develop critically needed commercial skills such as planning, financial management and marketing skills. The benefit for sponsoring companies is that they gain public recognition as good corporate citizens. The National Economic and Social Development Board (NESDB) of the Government has endorsed the TBIRD concept as one of several approaches for rural development.

The TBIRD concept has significant implications for both youth employment and youth participation in rural development because it exposes rural youth to the spirit of entrepreneurship, and demonstrates to them what it takes to be an independent economic entity utilizing human capital.

*Source:* *Business for development: the HRD approach of TBIRD; ESCAP, 1994.*

Youth policies encompass all facets of life and, for that reason, in addition to the integration of a youth policy into the overall national development framework, appropriate collaborative mechanisms should be put in place at the stage of policy formulation. Policy implementation requires concerted efforts by a number of ministries, agencies and non-governmental bodies. To bring about a collaborative relationship of that nature at the time of implementation, the formulation of policy documents should also involve appropriate consultation and collaboration among the various bodies concerned since they will have to work within the general framework of the national development policy. In this respect, it is noteworthy that the survey revealed that in many countries the youth policy formulation process involved a number of parties, most notably youth organizations (12 countries). According to the responses from other countries, Parliamentary Commissions, the judiciary, law enforcement, political parties, universities and research centres, religious and local communities, and local government had been involved in the youth policy formulation process.

This section has shown that in order for youth policy to be truly effective, youth policy should be developed as independent legislation, while at the same time, it should be closely integrated into the overall strategy for national development. Further, it is necessary to involve related agencies and ministries in the initial policy formulation stage in order to enlist collaboration of these agencies in the implementation stage.

## B. POLICY OBJECTIVES

Consensus building in setting the objectives and principles of a youth policy is the first step towards the formulation of a comprehensive national policy for youth. The major objectives of national youth policies in the ESCAP region may be categorized within the following five areas:

(1)    To develop the full potential of youth, spiritually, morally, intellectually, vocationally and physically in order to produce good citizens, leaders and preservers of cultural heritage;

(2)    To encourage active participation of youth in the socio-economic development of the country;

(3)   To provide support for youth groups movements and to support youth exchanges;

(4)   To provide protection and guidance for youth, especially for those in difficult circumstances, including economically disadvantaged families and juvenile delinquents;

(5)   To ensure the full rights of youth as members of society, including their rights to adequate shelter, education, employment opportunities, and all other civil and legal rights.

Almost all of the youth policies in the region appear to include objectives 1 and 2. While the first objective covers the general statement of the perception of youth, which is typically the recognition of youth as a human resource with high potential, the second objective defines the nature and extent of youth participation in society.  Within the framework of the Jakarta Plan of Action on Human Resources Development, the first objective relates to investment in human resources, while the second objective relates to the utilization of human resources and to the participation of those human resources in enhancing the quality of life. Therefore, the first two objectives are closely interrelated, as typified by the policy objective of Bangladesh: "to develop socio-economic conditions of youth and thereby transform unproductive youth into a productive human resource that accelerates the pace of national development".

However, it should be noted that the concept of "participation of youth in national development" should not be interpreted as a means of exploitation and utilization of youth human resources for national development.  It should rather imply the participation of youth themselves in the decision-making process of national development.   In other words, rather than perceiving youth from a purely objective perspective as resources for national development, it is important to view youth from a subjective perspective as stake-holders and members of society.  The policy objective of Malaysia clearly states this point and aims to instill positive individual characteristics of youth, so as to nurture a constructive leadership spirit among youth, as well as promote their participation in nation building at all levels. The planning and implementation process of the Malaysian national development plan includes a youth development component, as proposed by the Ministry of Youth and Sports.   The formulation of the country's youth policy involves consultations with the National

---

REVIEW OF THE YOUTH SITUATION, POLICIES AND PROGRAMMES
IN ASIA AND THE PACIFIC

Youth Consultative Council.  In other words, the youth policy of Malaysia, which focuses strongly on leadership development, has a system for nurturing leadership and aspirations among youth.  It ensures that the vision of tomorrow's leaders is reflected in today's national policy.

As a part of objective 1, many countries find fostering a cultural identity among youth to be important.  Many countries, including Indonesia, Maldives and Sri Lanka, include the preservation of cultural heritage and identity as an important role of youth in society.  Further, the Commonwealth of Independent States appears to have recognized the potential of youth, as indicated by the Government of Kazakstan, in the formulation of a national identity and ideology of the sovereign independent state, and in reviving a national ethos.

Objectives 3, 4 and 5 deal with the responsibilities of society towards youth.  Other forms of governmental service provided for youth, as a part of societal responsibilities, are included in some of the countries' policy objectives.  One example is the list of policy objectives of Guam, which include clear statements on governmental service provisions for youth:  (a) to provide youth services and programmes to all districts; (b) to encourage, through direct or indirect means, all youth, and especially those in need of guidance and motivation, to make use of existing youth facilities, services and programmes; (c) to establish a comprehensive approach to providing services and programmes for youth, taking into consideration the coordination and consolidation of existing programmes, services and planning with the implementation of new programmes and services where deemed necessary; and (d) to make such referrals as are necessary when certain services are best provided by other agencies within the Government of Guam or by other resources within the community or abroad.  A unique feature of these statements is that the Government of Guam clearly recognizes the importance of coordination on the part of the youth-related agencies in order to provide efficient services for youth.  It has thus incorporated "coordination" as a part of its policy objectives. The youth policy of Guam also includes another unique objective, namely collecting and disseminating information and research data relating to the needs and problems of youth, and keeping the Governor, the Judges of the Courts of Guam, the Guam Legislature, the District Commissioners and the general public informed of all major youth developments and achievements.

Japan has a specific policy for the prevention of juvenile delinquency, and specifies strengthening the collection and dissemination of information and research on juvenile delinquency as part of the youth policy for establishing a system of rehabilitation and preventive measures. The scarcity of information and research on youth is one of the main reasons for the present level of governmental commitment to youth issues. Strengthening information and research activities concerning youth should be an important service of a Government, particularly given the fact that the needs and profiles of youth are rapidly changing in the societies of today. Strengthening the information gathering and dissemination services in itself would serve to enhance the general awareness of any society regarding youth issues.

From the above, it may be concluded that most of the countries of the ESCAP region recognize youth as a positive force. As such, they are focusing their youth policy objectives on the development of the full potential of that portion of their human resource pool in order to ensure the maximum contribution of youth to the development of their societies. In that regard, most countries recognize the importance of providing a suitable environment for the active participation of youth in society. However, the concept of "participation" of youth seems to vary among the countries of the region. Only a limited number of countries clearly include participation of youth in the decision-making process as a part of the objectives of their youth policies. Further, only a few countries include societal responsibilities for youth in their policy objectives.

What appears to be lacking in many of the existing youth policies are strategies for promoting capacity-building governmental bodies and non-governmental organizations. Strong institutions, as well as links between them, are important for ensuring that the necessary mechanisms for youth development are established in society. Ideally, when there is an established concept of societal responsibility for youth development, resource mobilization for necessary action should come from society in general, rather than through dependence on a limited budget allocation for "youth affairs" from the central Government.

## C.  POLICY IMPLEMENTATION

### Institutions

There has been an increasing trend in the 1990s towards promoting national youth policies and programmes through a specific government ministry or department of youth. Almost 100 countries throughout the world have established such government ministries or departments of youth. Most of the respondents to the regional survey indicated that they had a national focal point ministry for the promotion of youth policies. Many countries have ministries of youth and sports, and some countries have established bodies to address youth matters within the presidential or prime minister's office (e.g., Japan, the Philippines, Sri Lanka, and Thailand).

In Sri Lanka, a commission on youth was appointed by the President to review the problems affecting young people, in cooperation with the Ministry of Youth Affairs and Sports, the National Youth Service Council and the National Apprentice Board. Their concern originated from the political upheaval of the relatively educated, unemployed youth, which caused serious tensions in society. As a result of the review, the governmental focal point agency for the development of youth was reorganized under the Ministry of Youth Affairs, Sports and Rural Development. By merging youth affairs with rural development, with its stronger financial backing and extensive grassroots level networks, the Ministry can formulate projects that extensively involve rural youth, which comprise nearly 80 per cent of the total youth population. A major project is "Samurdi (Prosperity)", the national poverty eradication programme, which is largely implemented by organized youth groups at the grassroots level.

In the majority of the countries and areas of the region, policies and programmes for youth are implemented by the ministries or departments which are responsible for integrating and coordinating such policies and programmes. In many countries, the Ministry of Youth and Sports is designated as the focal point for youth matters and entrusted with the coordinating role for all youth-related programmes, although the youth programme budget itself is allocated among several related ministries. In several other countries, the Ministry of Youth and Sports also assumes the responsibility of the only body dealing with youth matters, receiving the entire budget allocation.

Some countries have opted for establishment of national youth councils, which primarily function as the coordinating committee of organizations and institutions concerned with youth, but often with a high level of government authority. They are represented in various government sectors such as education and training, health and welfare, and are provided with the machinery to plan and coordinate the long-term development of a national youth policy. In addition, the national youth councils or institutes usually coordinate the work of all youth groups and youth organizations to encourage cooperation.

The National Youth Council of Singapore, for example, was given the key role of: (a) providing overviews of the important trends and situation of youth and recommending policy options accordingly; (b) initiating new programmes for youth to fill the gaps in existing programmes; and (c) coordinating programmes and activities of youth organizations. Another example is the Maldives Youth Council, which comprised all relevant government departments. In addition, there is a non-governmental counterpart of the Youth Council, the Youth Forum, which has as its members all registered youth clubs.

In India, the Government set up a National Youth Council with the support of Ministers from relevant Ministries, both at the state and central Government levels. The government also set up over 100 Nehru Yuvak Kendra (Nehru Youth Centres) all over the country with a central coordinating body; the government-controlled programmes for non-student youth development are carried out by the Nehru Youth Organizations. Separate from the governmental programme, there is also a national level coordinating committee of youth organizations, which is known as "National Committee of Youth Organizations in India (NCYOI)". There are four regional youth centres with staff of over 100 people. A wide range of programmes, including training, is being implemented by the member organizations of NCYOI.

In review, observance of the International Youth Year led to the establishment of a national focal point agency on youth affairs in many countries of the region. Most of those countries set up ministries of youth and sports to coordinate youth-related programmes. However, even with the establishment of such focal ministries, the national budget for youth-related programmes continued to be spread across a number of sectoral ministries. In other countries, a national youth council was appointed to

# Box 11. Youth development planning – Thailand

In an effort to mainstream youth policy in Thailand's overall national economic and social development plan, the period covered in the youth development plan coincides with that of the national development plan.

The focus of Thailand's Eighth National Economic and Social Development Plan (1997-2001) is human resources development. Problems faced by youth in difficult circumstances are specifically addressed in the five-year plan and emphasis has been placed on strengthening the functions of the family and community, and the development of youth from the earliest stages.

The planning process of the Eighth Five-Year Plan was significantly different from previous plans. This was the first time that the development of the plan involved two parallel process: governmental review and people's participation through NGOs. The two processes converged towards the conclusion of the planning process. The five-year plan development process comprised five stages, as illustrated below.

The youth development plan was also created by utilizing a similar process to that employed in the development of the national five-year plan. Essentially, the planning process involved two procedures: (a) the government process, coordinated by the National Youth Bureau, the highest government agency responsible for youth affairs; and (b) the non-governmental process, which aimed at coming up with an action plan at the grassroots level.

The government process started with an analysis of the desirable human qualities as identified in the eighth five-year plan. Then the strategies for developing these desirable qualities in youth were discussed at a series of 10 workshops in which government officials, NGO personnel, academics, media personnel, political figures, youth leaders and community leaders participated. The draft Youth Development Plan was also reviewed by a subcommittee comprising similar stakeholders prior to review by the Cabinet.

The non-governmental process started with a survey of the youth situation at the provincial level. First, 18 provinces were selected for the survey; experts and local NGOs that were to conduct the survey were identified. The preparation for, and the implementation of, the survey included: training of local NGOs; determination of scope and framework of the survey; preparation and field testing of the questionnaires; and interviews with 200 youth leaders in each province on their views regarding the situation and their suggested solutions to the problems. The exercise was also aimed at raising the awareness of the importance of local-level data collection as a basis for preparation of the youth development plan.

As a result of the survey, the need for the demarcation of roles as well as collaboration between central and local-level government and NGOs in tackling different issues were identified.

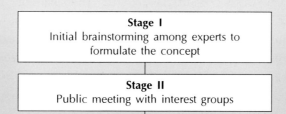

**Stage I**
Initial brainstorming among experts to formulate the concept

**Stage II**
Public meeting with interest groups

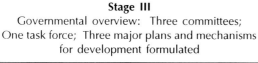

**Stage III**
Governmental overview: Three committees;
One task force; Three major plans and mechanisms
for development formulated

**Stage III**
People's participation process:
Nine subregions; Ten major development
strategies

**Stage IV**
Merging the results of the two processes to produce the draft five-year plan

**Stage V**
Review meeting to produce the final draft

coordinate youth programmes. A sufficient degree of success was achieved by these national youth councils, as a major part of their work was to coordinate the activities of non-governmental youth organizations.

Based on the past regional experience, it may be concluded that the organizational location, that is, the level of government authority attached to the focal point agency, together with the level of budgetary support, are critical factors that influence the effectiveness of the agency as a coordinating body.

### Translation of policy into programmes

According to a 1992 report by the Commonwealth Secretariat, a "youth policy should spell out only the broad parameters of work and the general outline of action so that the implementing agencies, especially the NGOs, have adequate scope and freedom to evolve their own programmes and activities on the basis of their philosophy of work, objectives, needs of the beneficiary groups and position of resources". By setting up a clear but broad framework  for programme development, a youth policy serves as an effective instrument for mobilizing the different parties concerned in a country, particularly youth organizations, in planning and implementing youth programmes.

For example, the Ministry of Youth and Sports of Malaysia set out guidelines for the development of, and participation in, programmes by youth organizations in the Rakan Muda (Young Partners) Programme. The guidelines set forth the mission of the Ministry and the goals of the Rakan Muda Programme, together with the roles of the Ministry, NGOs and the private sector, the procedure for receiving financial assistance and the specific criteria for programme development. The guidelines clearly state that the success of the entire programme depends largely on the networking and complementary and collaborative activities of the Ministry and NGOs.

The major goal of the Rakan Muda Programme is to minimize the unproductive use of time by youth and to develop youth in accordance with the national development perception of "Vision 2020". Accordingly, the Ministry sets the criteria for the participating programmes, which include: (a) optimizing the free time available among youth who participate in the programmes, so that they do not become involved in wasteful and immoral activities; (b) maximizing the contributions by youths to their peers and society at large, and developing their potential as productive citizens; (c) enlarging the membership of relevant NGOs and enhancing their programme of activities; (d) maximizing the social and economic contributions of NGOs and youth for the social, economic and cultural transformation of the country; and (e) enhancing the positive attitude of youth, developing their mind set and world view and stimulating group efforts by youth to improve the organizations to which they belong. The guidelines list 10 categories of activities (sports, martial arts, environment, culture and arts, innovation, entrepreneurship, physical fitness, community service, recreation and uniformed corps), under which the NGOs may formulate specific programmes for implementation.

In short, it should be noted by policy makers that an "enabling" environment can be created by the articulation of a broad but clear policy framework that allows room for flexibility in programme development to tap the creative talents of the concerned parties involved in youth affairs, particularly youth NGOs. The important role of youth policy, in addition to providing an overall framework and direction for youth activities, is to promote the involvement of a wide range of actors, including government, NGOs, the private sector and youth themselves.

## Coordination issues

As discussed under section A of this chapter on policy formulation, the implementation of a national youth policy requires close coordination among all the parties concerned. A typical case appears to involve more than five ministries, while in the case of Indonesia, 20 government departments are involved in implementation. Implementation often involves budget distribution among the ministries involved and only a few countries and areas (Bangladesh, Fiji, and Hong Kong) indicated that their total youth programme budgets were consolidated under one ministry or agency.

In most countries, the coordination task of the youth affairs focal point goes far beyond the ministries. For example, in the case of Fiji, the Ministry of Youth advocates intersectoral cooperation in promoting youth participation; thus it networks with NGOs such as the Young Men's Christian Association (YMCA), the Young Women's Christian Association (YWCA), Provincial Youth Councils, Boy Scouts and Girl Guides. In the private sector, the Government works with banks, companies and industries to promote the Youth Careers' Exposition. The Ministry also works with individual students, schools, religious groups and international organizations to promote youth participation in development. In Bangladesh, the role of NGOs is viewed as complementary to the governmental programmes. The Government thus encourages NGO participation in related activities and provides financial assistance.

---

## Box 12. Organizational location of the youth focal point agency

John Ewen, the author of the UNESCO publication "Guidance on National Youth Policy", suggests six options for the location of a youth focal point office, each of which reflects the political commitment of the Government. He argues that the location of such an office, and its ministerial level, influences the success or failure of the functions of that office.

Ewen explains that cross-sectoral offices such as a youth affairs office tend to have a weaker position in coordination efforts because they do not possess a bargaining position similar to that of the "traditional" cross-sectoral ministries such as the Treasury, Finance Ministry or ministries involved in planning and development. The sectoral ministries have to take these "traditional" cross-sectoral ministries seriously because the former depends on

the latter for budget allocations and approvals of projects. In other words, the sectoral ministries need their cross-sectoral counterparts to do their job. However, the sectoral ministries do not have a similar relationship with the new breed of cross-sectoral ministries such as those dealing with youth, women, the elderly and children's affairs. The sectoral ministries do not have to seek either approval or budget allocations from the new breed of ministries. Therefore, in order for these new cross-sectoral ministries to successfully "coordinate" with the sectoral ministries, they need to position themselves strategically. The degree of likelihood of success of that such cross-sectoral ministries may achieve in relation to their "positioning" within the governmental structure is illustrated below.

### Ladder of potential success of a cross-sectoral unit

| | | |
|---|---|---|
| **Maximum** | 1. | Office located in Prime Minister's Secretariat, with a minister assisting the Prime Minister |
| | 2. | Separate ministry with powerful Minister holding another key portfolio, e.g., Deputy Prime Minister or Defence Minister |
| | 3. | Division of an important key ministry (e.g., employment, education and training) under a senior minister |
| **Probability of successful coordination** | 4. | Separate ministry under a junior minister |
| **Minimum** | 5. | Combined ministry (e.g., women and culture, youth and sport) with low status functions under a junior minister |
| | 6. | Part of a rag-bag ministry with a variety of ill-fitting low status functions (e.g., youth, sport, culture and tourism) |

*Source:* Youth Studies Australia; 14:3, Spring 1995.

In Malaysia, the Government is aiming to ensure coordination among the different sectors with the introduction of the Rakan Muda Programme, the establishment of an information coordination and implementation network comprising government agencies, NGOs and the private sector at the State, national and district levels. There is a formal national level coordinating mechanism for youth affairs in Malaysia, known as the National Youth Consultative Committee (NYCC). All important matters concerning youth are determined through the NYCC, which consists of both the government and NGOs; NYCC is thus a vehicle to enable collaboration between the Ministry and youth NGOs.

In Singapore, the National Youth Council (NYC) is the national coordinating body for youth affairs, and as such it networks and coordinates the programmes of the various participating groups. NYC also manages some programmes directly and involves the participating groups in the development of national and international programmes and activities for youth.

In terms of legislation, Thailand has a number of Acts which ensure coordination: the National Youth Promotion and Co-ordination Act, the National Declaration on Children, the National Plan of Action, and the Child and Youth Development Plan. In Mongolia, the Union of Young Mongolian Revolutionaries formerly had full authority for implementing youth policy. However, with the transition to a democratic political structure, a number of different organizations have emerged to deal with youth issues, including the Youth Department, NGOs, and youth and students' organizations. At present, the Mongolian Youth Federation plays an important role among youth NGOs, as it has full government recognition.

Coordination between government and non-governmental organizations is also necessary in order to avoid duplication of work. In that regard, it is regrettable to note that many of the national coordination committees created specifically to undertake preparations for International Youth Year were disbanded after commemoration of the Year. This may have resulted from a failure by countries to recognize the importance of coordination in securing effective integration of youth policies into development planning.

From the above, it is clear that extensive coordination is the key to the effective implementation of youth policies in any country. However, experience has shown that the task of coordinating has been an overwhelming function for the national focal point agency, given that most are newly established and lack strong financial backing. In this connection, it may be useful to note the suggestions of the 1993 study by the United Nations on the global situation of youth in the 1990. The study points out that basic conditions have to be fulfilled in order for coordination mechanisms to function effectively. These include: (a) an adequate commitment to, and adequate instruments for, furthering youth policy objectives; (b) a capacity to coordinate ongoing activities and to identify areas requiring attention and developmental effort; and (c) development of the proper organizational balance by sufficient government, non-governmental and youth representation.

## Major difficulties encountered in youth policy implementation

In addition to the issues of coordination discussed above, many countries of the ESCAP region appear to share five major obstacles in the implementation of youth policies.

The first obstacle is inadequate legislation and policy direction for youth development. Some countries pointed out that the lack of a clear policy document setting out the priority areas and direction for youth development was still a major constraint. A few countries indicated that a lack of legislation defining the institutional relationship between youth-related governmental organizations and NGOs was an obstacle.

The second obstacle observed is the issue of human resources for youth policy implementation. Many responses to the survey expressed concern over the inadequate quality of personnel from youth ministries and the scarcity of training opportunities available to them. Another issue involving human resources was reported to be the scarcity of youth leaders at various levels.

The third constraint is the issue of inadequate financial support for youth policy implementation. This appears to be an obstacle common among most of the countries of the region. As noted above, the youth budget appears to be typically shared among a number of ministries in order to facilitate coordination and collaboration in youth policy implementation. However, sharing a small pie often makes it difficult to achieve the effective implementation of operational activities.

The fourth obstacle is the difficulty experienced in identifying the common needs of youth. The issue sometimes results from the wide variation in the definition of youth in a number of countries in the region. The needs of youth aged 15 to 40 years are, obviously, quite different in their nature. In other countries, the issues have more to do with the heterogeneous nature of youth due to the differences in their economic status and other socio-cultural characteristics. However, quite apart from the varied needs among different subgroups of youth, the lack of up-to-date baseline data on such needs in general is considered a major constraint.

The fifth issue concerns the lack of a systematic monitoring and evaluation process in many countries. For example, the Government of Sri Lanka conducts evaluations of youth policy through discussions with youth representatives at the national, provincial and grassroots levels. Although the value of such an exercise is fully recognized, it is also felt that the application of common evaluation criteria is difficult because of the wide range of youth projects carried out by the variety of bodies. The results of these activities are often recorded in qualitative but not quantitative terms. Therefore, the measurement of the aggregate effect of a youth policy often becomes difficult.

## D. OBSERVATIONS

One strategy advocated during the International Youth Year: Participation, Development, Peace was the need to establish appropriate coordination mechanisms within each country in order to encourage the integration of youth issues into overall national development planning. In response to this advocacy, numerous Governments in the region formulated youth policies and created ministries, councils, departments, secretariats and offices which, in many cases were granted a high level of government authority to promote and implement national youth policies.

However, the mechanisms for implementing youth policies appear to be in need of review in many countries. Ministries or departments responsible for youth affairs are often charged with responsibility for developing policies and programmes which address the mass of unemployed out-of-school youth, while being left in weak financial and political positions with regard to the coordination of youth activities with other line ministries and NGOs. Even when the coordination efforts with other ministries are successful, the necessary support is only provided when surplus resources are available after each sectoral ministry has implemented its own programmes. Therefore, in many countries where strong political commitment is absent, youth ministries tend to limit themselves to peripheral activities concerning youth: recreation, culture, sports and mobilization of youth organizations for specific projects. While the creation of youth ministries and equivalent agencies is, in a sense, a manifestation of government support for youth development, the strategic positioning of such institutions, together with adequate financial backing, appears essential to their full and effective functioning.

Efforts should also be made to ensure better coordination, not only among government agencies but also between government agencies and NGOs. Existing youth organizations need to be further developed. Non-governmental youth organizations have played a key role in reaching out to young people with programmes and services as well as in representing their interests. A youth policy should aim, *inter alia,* towards the promotion of non-governmental youth organizations, by setting up a clear framework for their activities. Youth organizations should not be viewed merely as an arm of governmental organizations to be used in reaching the youth population. A youth policy should actually be structured in such a way as to encourage creativity and initiative of youth organizations. Governmental support for youth organizations could take a variety of forms and not just be limited to financial assistance. Such support could be in the form of services and expertise in the planning and implementation of the organizations' activities, bearing in mind the need to maintain the independence of such organizations. One method would be to support a network of youth organizations as a forum for exchanging views and experiences, and for providing opportunities for resource sharing.

Again, while a number of initiatives have been taken in the Asian and Pacific region during the course of the decade following International Youth Year, many countries have only begun to take action to set up youth policies, and youth ministries and agencies in the 1990s. In addition, the newly developed youth policies have yet to be fully integrated into the overall national development strategies. Youth policies are among the newest type of legislation in many countries of the region, and there is a high demand for regional sharing of experience in their formulation and implementation. The possibilities for regional cooperation in this field, particularly through networking of youth organizations, both governmental and non-governmental, are tremendous. The time is ripe for governments and NGOs to forge ahead with such initiatives.

# Part Two:

# INNOVATIVE PROGRAMMES OF YOUTH ORGANIZATIONS

# Education

# I

## A. PROJECT HOPE

### China Youth Development Foundation and
### All-China Youth Federation

Project Hope was established by the China Youth Development Foundation to provide opportunities for primary education to young people in the poorest counties of China. To ensure effective implementation of the project at all levels, the Foundation teamed up with the All-China Youth Federation (ACYF), a semi-government youth body which had branches at the national, provincial, regional, county and community levels.

The main mission of Project Hope is to address the problem of primary school-dropouts among "poor" children, numbering approximately one million per year. Using survey techniques to identify the specific target group and assess the extent and nature of problems in every village in the poorer counties, Project Hope seeks to return children to schools, where possible, and to prevent drop-outs from occurring in high-risk circumstances. This is essentially achieved by financing, through voluntary contributions, a child's school fees for five years.

Results indicate that Project Hope represents a highly successful and cost-effective way of upgrading primary school retention, and thus promoting literacy among poor children. So far, 860,000 children in 1,200 counties in 30 provinces have been assisted. Almost 100 per cent of these children go on to complete primary school.

A second aim of Project Hope is to improve the primary school facilities where the assisted children are taught. School buildings are often unsafe, not rainproof, lack electricity, and are run-down to the point that they detract from the students' learning capacity. Project Hope contributes towards rectifying that situation, while inspiring others to play a role in doing so.

Project Hope has already established 300 new primary schools, named "Hope Schools". The construction of a "Hope School" is subject to conditions set by the Project. For instance, the Project provides only a proportion of the total cost of each school, with the balance coming from local funds, and communal and private donations. The site for the schools must be provided by the local county government or the public, while labour and materials for construction must be provided free or at minimal cost. These conditions ensure that a village receives a new school only when its own willingness to contribute are apparent, thus ensuring communal commitment to the school. The expectation is for the local people to not only to build the school but to maintain it, and supply it with teachers, thus ensuring its long-term viability.

As reflected in its name, Project Hope seeks not only to offer hope to individuals, but also to the community in general, through the provision of primary education opportunities for children living in poverty. Project Hope conveys to families and communities the message that the education of their children is a critical to the overall development of their families and communities. It seeks to encourage local government, communities and families to take what initiative they can in ensuring the education of their children as an investment in the future.

As a way of ensuring community participation, the Foundation established the Project in such a way that its operations would be almost entirely dependent on voluntary contributions, in an environment where such practice is not common among the people. It is significant to note that despite great odds the Foundation chose to rely on this approach to raise funds, which was extremely demanding in terms of time and energy, rather than seek international assistance.

Project Hope adopts a decentralized approach to project implementation to maximize participation by the local people. This ensures the responsiveness of the Project to local needs and conveys to the local people a sense of project ownership. The headquarters of Project Hope is located in Beijing in the China Youth Development Foundation. With a staff of 40, consisting mainly of young people, the headquarters is pivotal in maintaining a steady inflow of donations and in ensuring that funds are utilized in response to the specific needs of communities. The headquarters also plays an important role in maintaining accountability to all parties through both internal and external audits as well as by holding of donor consultations.

On the other hand, the success of Project Hope ultimately depends on the work undertaken at the local level. Through teaming up with the All-China Youth Federation, which has extensive outreach in the country, the Foundation has been able to maintain a decentralized administrative structure for implementation of project activities. ACYF provides full staffing support to Project Hope at all levels of operation: provincial, regional, county and local.

It is the ACYF staff who undertake the technical work of Project Hope. They carry out local surveys of students, compile lists of those seeking or needing Project Hope assistance, make visits to monitor and check on the progress of assisted students, and generally promote all related work at the local level. The Project Hope staff are closely integrated within their local communities, which has the effect of making the whole project a local enterprise.

It is the local project staff who receive requests for assistance, hold discussions with schools and the village leadership, and finally compile a list of needed action for submission to county level government authorities. The county government and education commission review the list and try to secure available county funds or raise private funds locally to address some of the needs on the list. They in turn submit a streamlined list of remaining needs to a regional office that oversees a number of counties. At the regional level, some assistance may then be made available for specific needs. Then, finally, a further revised list goes to headquarters. Once the requests have been matched with available resources, the various levels are again involved in reverse order. In that way, specific needs are "owned" and addressed by the different levels of the Project's operations.

The success of this strategy is reflected in several ways: (a) the local "branches" of Project Hope are able to raise money locally; (b) local government addresses some of the needs identified but not met by Project Hope; (c) communities manage to provide matching grants and labour for Project Hope ventures.

Through teaming up with ACYF which has enabled Project Hope to adopt a decentralized approach to project administration, a sense of community ownership of the Project has been generated. While the project receives no government financial assistance, it enjoys strong government support. Leading Chinese statesmen, including Premier Deng Xiaoping, have given their personal support to the Project. The Education Commission works closely with the Foundation at all levels, while local government is a very strong supporter of the work in tangible ways.

In short, although it is an NGO, the China Youth Development Foundation and its Project Hope are deeply rooted in China's governmental and communal systems.

## B.  CHILD WELFARE LAWS PROJECT

### Child Welfare Association of Thailand

The Child Welfare Laws Project was initiated in 1986 by the Child Welfare Association of Thailand to disseminate information and improve existing laws to protect the rights and welfare of children. During its early years, the Project produced the Child Welfare Laws Handbook, and conducted seminars and workshops to disseminate relevant information. The initial target groups of the Project were adults, child welfare workers, and concerned officials of government agencies and NGOs.

In 1990, under the Project, the Association started the "Legal Literacy for Rural Children" initiative. The premise of the project was that child welfare laws could not become fully effective unless the children and youth themselves were made to understand those laws. The project was directed at rural youth, as they constituted the majority of the young population of Thailand and were more vulnerable to exploitation as compared to their urban counterparts. The objectives of the project were to make rural youth more aware of their legal rights, and better equipped with legal knowledge to prevent them from being exploited.

The Young Farmers Groups were selected as the target group for the project.  This organization, which had representation in all the villages of the country, comprised children and youth  aged from 10 to 25 years. Of the total membership, 30 per cent were aged 10 to 14 years and 70 per cent were aged 15 to 25 years.

The Young Farmers Groups were already involved in community development work in their respective rural communities, with the support of the community leaders such as the village headmen, monks and teachers.  It was estimated that there were about 6,000 groups with a total of 200,000 members when the project started. Selected leaders and members of the Young Farmers Groups were provided with training.  Among those selected, one-third were aged below 14 years and one-third were between 15 and 25 years in age; the remainder comprised group advisors and included village headmen, teachers and women farmers.  During the three-year duration of the project, about 600 such individuals received training.

The Child Welfare Association of Thailand approached the Faculty of Law at Chulalongkorn University for collaboration in the implementation of this project. Students at the Faculty of Law were actively involved in the transfer of legal knowledge to less fortunate rural youth.  In fact, the training evaluations indicated great benefit for the law students as well as for the young farmers.  The project provided the young farmers with knowledge and understanding of child welfare and related laws applicable to everyday life.

The young farmers were also trained to disseminate this legal information in their own communities.  The law students benefited from the opportunity to use their knowledge and transfer it to others.  This was found to be an excellent form of apprenticeship, which resulted in practical skills enhancement.  The concept of youth helping youth to improve rural communities and to bring about the self-development of each other created a close relationship and understanding between the two groups.  This, in turn, led to stronger ties between the rural and urban communities.

The project was supported by other governmental and non-governmental agencies, including the Department of Agricultural Extension, the Forestry Department, the Department of Public Prosecution, the Revenue Court, the Labour Court, the Bangkok Metropolitan Administration, the Thai Yuwakasetkorn Promotion Foundation, the National Youth Bureau, the National Council for Child and Youth Development, the Law Office, the Girl Guides Association of Thailand and the World Health Organization.

In particular, the Department of Agricultural Extension was the main partner in implementing the project together with the Faculty of Law at Chulalongkorn University. Its involvement was important for the dissemination of information, and for ensuring the sustainability of the project through the incorporation of certain activities into the regular operations of the Department, including radio programmes for young farmers, training and workshops for young farmer leaders, and community services by Young Farmers Groups.

In the third year of the project, efforts were made to mainstream legal literacy initiatives. The National Farm Youth Development Plan for 1992-1996, which was developed, included the provision of legal literacy training through the Young Farmers Groups as a strategy to develop agricultural community leaders. Since the official commitment of the Government made it possible to institutionalize these legal training activities, specific strategies were developed and implemented under the project.

The experimental activities included: (a) the mobilization of local Agricultural Extension Agents and Young Farmers Groups' advisors to participate in the training activities; (b) the production of radio programmes, one for each aspect of law covered in the training sessions, which were broadcast weekly through the Department of Agricultural Extension to members of the Young Farmers Groups; (c) the incorporation of legal literacy components in events for young farmers at the local, provincial, regional and national levels through involving law students and trained young farmers.

At the community level, 40 trained and highly motivated farmers, who possessed sufficient legal knowledge to conduct local legal literacy activities, became the legal focal points. Recognition of the role of these legal focal points was accorded by other agencies. For example, Pollwatch, the authorized election monitoring group, appointed them as election watchdogs during the general election in March 1992. The focal points also organized pro-democracy activities in their own villages prior to the election, an experience which provided them with skills in project planning and management with local participation. In all of the 19 local legal literacy activities implemented during the last year of the project, those 40 legal focal points were the main driving force in conducting the courses.

The project was found to be sustainable for two main reasons. The first was the success in institutionalizing the project activities, which were integrated into the work of the Department of Agricultural Extension. The second was the desire of the law students and young farmers to continue their informal exchanges. Since the law students were readily accessible to the young farmers, the peer exchange did not suffer from the "barriers" which often occur between service providers and recipients in technical assistance projects. The contact between the participating urban and rural youth  has continued beyond the project period and has been a major factor in the successful establishment of cooperative ties between the two groups.

# Health                                        II

## A.  DEVELOPMENT OF FAMILY LIFE EDUCATION FOR YOUTH PROJECTS

### Family Planning Association of the Philippines

The population of the Philippines continues to grow at a rapid rate of 2.3 per cent annually; the country has the highest fertility rate in South-East Asia.  Over 5 million married women are in need of birth spacing or control. Socio-cultural factors inhibit family planning practice.  The low rate of contraceptive use at 36 per cent partly reflects that situation.

There are other statistics that indicate the unsatisfactory status of reproductive health among Filipino women.  Filipino mothers at high risk in childbearing constitute 63 per cent of the country's women of reproductive age, half of whom suffer from anaemia. Each year 1,600 women die of pregnancy-related causes.  In addition, a significant number of unsafe abortions have led to maternal deaths.

Young people in the Philippines are becoming sexually active at a younger age.  This trend hinders efforts to improve the reproductive health situation of the country. While there are a number of sex education programmes for youth, they are limited in scope.

A 1995 study on youth fertility by the University of the
Philippines revealed that almost one out of four young males had
paid for sex at least once and that the highest proportion who had
done so were in the youngest group aged 15 to 17 years. It was
also found that condom use was minimal among male youth who
had engaged in casual intercourse with sex workers during the 12
months preceding the study.

Against this background, the Family Planning Association of the
Philippines (FPOP) has been operating the Development and Family
Education for Youth (DAFLEY) project since 1983. The objectives
of the project are to provide: (a) a comprehensive package of
information, education, counseling and reproductive health services
which are designed to help youth understand the adverse
consequences of teenage pregnancy and early marriage; and (b)
livelihood skills training for out-of-school youths.

The project has two major components; one is the provision of
services through the Teen Centre and the other through outreach
activities. The Teen Centre, which is the base of the project in
Davao, undertakes a variety of activities. The Centre is equipped
with recreational facilities and a mini-library, which are open for
daily use. The receiving room, equipped with audio-visual facilities
and indoor games, are used for group discussions, meetings, and
social events.

Separate rooms are provided for counseling and telephone hotline
services are run by well-trained youth volunteers. Counseling is
undertaken in a private room to ensure confidentiality, while
the hotline telephone service is available for youth who prefer
anonymous counseling. The latter service provides alternative
modes of counseling.

The volunteers at the Centre also produce educational materials
concerning youth health which they disseminate widely to young
people. Another means of information dissemination undertaken by
the Centre is through its newsletter, *Peryodikit*, which highlights
activities conducted by the Teen Centre.

In addition to the activities at the Teen Centre, a number of
outreach activities are carried out, including: (a) income generation
activities, for which loans are provided to selected trained youth
to initiate income generating projects such as raising livestock; and
(b) community activities such as sports, as a way of effectively
reaching youth.

Implementation of the DAFLEY project is heavily reliant on youth volunteers, making it a youth-to-youth scheme. The project, which has received many awards, has served successfully as a centre for adolescents to obtain information and advice about their reproductive health.

## B.    HIV/AIDS CAMPAIGN

### Indian Committee of Youth Organizations

The Indian Committee of Youth Organization[1] (ICYO) is a non-profit, non-governmental organization committed to developing mutual cooperation and understanding among the different voluntary youth agencies, organizations, associations, groups and clubs that function in India. The objective of ICYO is to strengthen the existing youth agencies and foster the development of new agencies in the areas of youth mobilization for environmental preservation, rural community development, health, population, and cultural and national development.

Concerned with the threat of AIDS to young people, ICYO started campaigning to sensitize and mobilize people to implement AIDS prevention programmes in October 1987. The World Assembly of Youth (WAY) had at that time involved a number of youth organizations in the public debate on drug abuse prevention. AIDS was then not a topic for open discussion in India.

Recognizing that the participation of youth was essential for preventing the spread of HIV/AIDS, an intercountry workshop was organized in collaboration with the World Health Organization and WAY for the South and South-East Asian regions. Doctors, researchers, social workers and youth workers discussed the need to develop strategies for combating the epidemic of HIV/AIDS.

ICYO learned about the reaction of young people to the epidemic through the workshop and explored ways of developing interventions by youth for youth. The workshop confirmed that there was enough capacity among youth NGOs to carry out

---

[1]    Details are based on *HIV and AIDS Responses of Youth – Learning Experiences from Macro and Micro Interventions by Youth*, Akash Gualia, Indian Committee of Youth Organizations, 1994.

work on HIV/AIDS prevention. It was also felt that youth could play a role in protecting AIDS victims from stigmatization and discrimination. Fifteen youth action plans for combating HIV/ AIDS were finalized at the workshop, including advocacy utilizing the mass media through information, education and communication strategies, and by identifying different strategies for different target groups (urban youth, rural youth and hard-to-reach youth, such as young sex workers and street children).

In June 1992, ICYO decided to focus on the twin epidemics of drugs and HIV/AIDS in a concerted manner, fully mobilizing its network at the grassroots and international levels. The first set of activities was a campaign to sensitize the workers of the member youth organizations to the need to learn about AIDS and include components of HIV/AIDS prevention education in their programmes. ICYO produced two sets of posters for this purpose. The first poster carried the message: "Youth campaign to contain deadly HIV virus" and an illustration of four hands clutching each other, symbolizing solidarity, strength and mutual respect. The poster also carried a gender sensitive message with two hands wearing bangles, indicating the equal participation of women, mutual respect and sensitivity towards the problem, and gender issues involved in HIV/AIDS prevention education. The results from pre-testing the posters were good.

A separate set of posters has been prepared which target semi-literate and illiterate youth in rural and urban communities. In addition to disseminating the posters, the ICYO documentation centre collects books, journals, newspapers, pamphlets, videos, reports and periodicals on the subject, which are made available to youths. ICYO also introduced its services to subscribers of its newsletter by inserting a one-page announcement of the AIDS prevention campaign.

Further, in order to reach out to the most vulnerable segment of the population, a few small community-based formal and informal groups were constituted, comprising residents of the slums in New Delhi. This exercise was aimed at testing the validity of the ICYO strategies on small and informal groups.

The first one-day workshop for youth NGOs was organized in April 1993, in which 12 youth NGOs participated. The programme provided the youth leaders of the local NGOs with knowledge, skills and self-confidence for communicating with their peers about HIV/AIDS.

The various organizations prepared action plans based on the needs of their own community. Some organizations suggested mass education programmes, while others came up with innovative ideas for communicating with hard-to-reach groups and popularizing the use of condoms. Groups developed innovative methods of spreading the message, including street plays, puppets, "AIDS Game" and "Condom Dip", a game that provides winners with free packets of condoms.

At the same time, ICYO conducted a series of consultations with youth leaders to formulate effective means of communication and programme development for AIDS prevention. The consultations facilitated the generation of new ideas, while also helping to reduce fears and overcome emotional and social barriers among the participating youth leaders. Further, it helped the participants to gain more knowledge about AIDS and motivated them to work on various aspects of the HIV/AIDS problem.

ICYO has generated impressive results, including finalizing the Youth Agenda for South and South-East Asia and the initiation of national activities based on the Youth Agenda, the strengthening of documentation on HIV/AIDS, the preparation of campaign materials including posters, street plays and AIDS games, the creation of a network among youth NGOs and the introduction of peer educators. As the next step, ICYO plans to set up drop-in centres to provide information, advice and reassurance to people concerned about AIDS-related issues in slum areas. It is also planning to start AIDS-prevention training programmes, including one targeted for women.

# Employment III

## A. SKILLS DEVELOPMENT AND JOB PROMOTION PROGRAMMES

### Vietnam Youth Federation

The Vietnam Youth Federation (VYF), an NGO based in Hanoi, works specifically for the welfare of youth in Viet Nam. The Federation's activities focus on providing educational as well as employment opportunities for rural youth through providing scholarships, financial assistance and credit for young people, especially those living under difficult circumstances.

Already, scholarship funds have been established in 38 cities/provinces 17,706 scholarships have been provided to young people. The Federation has established 2,935 youth socio-economic programmes and projects with a total input value of Dong 59.3 billion, involving the participation of some 100,000 young people in 53 cities/provinces.

More directly, with the aim of creating opportunities for youth to find employment, the Federation has been providing them with appropriate training. The Federation has set up a network of some 200 offices for skills training and job promotion, where 92,000 youths have been trained. The innovation of these programmes is that the Federation not only provides skills training for youth, but also links the skills learned with the available jobs in the market.

In order to better serve the needs of rural youth, the Federation
has also set up a training programme that accommodates the
agricultural cycle. It has become increasingly difficult for youth
to economically sustain themselves with income from farming.
Finding jobs during the off-season period is, therefore, becoming
important for young people in rural areas. However, these
rural youths do not usually have marketable skills to enable them
to find employment right away. Hence, an appropriate scheduling
of training courses for these youth to fill the gap is one of the
most important mandates of the Federation.

The Federation has established an extensive network, particularly
in the rural areas, in order to be in direct touch with rural youth
and to be responsive to their needs. The Youth Volunteer Teams
were established to improve the responsiveness of the Federation to
the needs of rural youth. One of the aims of the programme is to
provide employment to jobless rural youth.

In the programme, rural youth have been taken into the Youth
Volunteer Teams and sent to other parts of the country where they
are hired to undertake various activities, just as breeding livestock
and tree planting. After three to five years of trial work, they (and
their families) may choose to stay on for a longer period, if they
wish to do so. This grassroots movement has been established in
14 cities/provinces and now has a membership of 150,000 youths.

Apart from the above services, the Federation has also initiated an
innovative scheme under which it encourages successful youth
entrepreneurs to impart their knowledge and experience to those
youth who have just started their own businesses and to assist
them through providing loans. This scheme also includes an
element of mutual assistance among the youths themselves for career
development. Real-life examples of successful peers serve as the
most effective form of motivation for young people. It should
be noted that many successful entrepreneurs in Viet Nam were in
fact recipients of the Federation's assistance.

The Federation has also taken advantage of the more favourable
economic environment which now exists in Viet Nam. It has taken
the initiative in mobilizing youth participation in socio-economic
development projects throughout the country. For example, youth
have contributed to the construction of the infrastructure that is

essential for the well-being of the rural poor. Aside from making a significant contribution to the country's development through this activity, the rural unemployed youths have also benefited from the resultant employment opportunities.

The Federation has also been successful in strengthening its financial position. Funds for specific programmes have grown; there has been an increase in the number of scholarships and prizes awarded to top students. The successful implementation of programmes by the Federation has also helped in capturing the attention of various organizations, which, in turn, has helped to further expand the financial basis of the Federation.

## B. SKILLS DEVELOPMENT PROGRAMME/ COMMONWEALTH YOUTH CREDIT INITIATIVE

### National Youth Congress of Solomon Islands

The Solomon Islands National Youth Congress is a quasi-governmental organization which is responsible for youth affairs. The organization's major activity is to fund projects directed towards youth development. It provides training especially for out-of-school youth and also initiates income-generating projects in rural areas. Training is organized with the help of private companies which is the major source of strength of this operation. Many of the projects were started a few years ago, and their full impact has yet to be seen. However, even at this stage, the organization is exerting a systematic effort to link all important resources for the employment of youths.

The organization is committed to the promotion of youth employment through various activities. Among the particularly relevant activities that it promotes is the National Skills Development Programme, which is intended to provide skills oriented towards employment for out-of-school youths aged 15 to 20 years. Mechanical, electrical, carpentry and plumbing skills are covered in the training course. The provision of initial capital through an award scheme, practical assistance in preparing job applications and interview training are also important components of the course.

The organization has successfully linked-up with private companies in the provision of economically-relevant training and support. For example, Solomon Telekom Company has started offering a course on electronics for out-of-school youths. Public and private links are essential, particularly in areas where training has to be effectively linked to job opportunities in the private sector. An innovative scheme is also offered which trains and supports youth volunteers working for community development in the villages. Training is offered not only for youth who want jobs in the private sector, but also for those who want to enter the public sector for further community development work.

The National Youth Congress was recently selected as the partner NGO in the youth credit scheme developed by the Commonwealth Youth Programme (CYP). Lack of access to credit often impedes self-help initiatives by young people to deal with unemployment. Simply because they do not possess any land or assets, youth are often unable to provide the collateral required for obtaining credit from formal sector financial institutions.

The Commonwealth Youth Credit Initiative (CYCI) was established by an expert group meeting, convened by CYP in 1994 in order to alleviate such bottlenecks in the development of young entrepreneurs. By helping to create a credit delivery system for young entrepreneurs, CYP has targeted a group often marginalized in development thinking and practice. CYCI aims to challenge conventional notions about young people and offer them the alternative of self-employment. Participants with a wide range of experience in youth and credit met in Malta to finalize a document which provided the framework for an agreement between CYP regional centres and NGOs who will operate the youth credit programme.

CYCI is designed to help young entrepreneurs who want to establish micro-enterprises to gain access to credit. The enterprises might be urban or rural, agricultural or non-agricultural, in the formal or informal sector. CYCI is being implemented as part of a package of measures to be taken by the Commonwealth Youth Programme that are required to enable the effective and sustainable development of small-scale enterprises. In addition, provision of a credit facility, other measures include entrepreneurship training, support service provisions, marketing assistance and information dissemination.

The youth credit scheme, finalized at the Malta meeting, is at present in the pilot project stage in four locations, and will be run over a three-year period. Solomon Islands is one of the four pilot locations together with Guyana, India and Zambia. The Solomon Islands programme commenced in Guadalcanal Province in its first year of operation and has been extended to other provinces for the second and third years of the programme. Any young person or youth organization that meets the target group criteria set forth under CYCI is eligible to become a borrower.

As the NGO partner, the National Youth Congress operates throughout Solomon Islands using its existing network to ensure effective functioning of the projects. The CYP South Pacific Centre provides external monitoring and evaluation support, seeks funding and co-financing of projects, makes available training manuals and training expertise, and assists in identifying other agencies that could contribute to the provision of support services. The National Youth Congress, in collaboration with the CYP South Pacific Centre, intends to disseminate and replicate the CYCI project model elsewhere in the region.

# Effective Participation IV

## A. FORMULATION OF MALAYSIA'S NEW NATIONAL YOUTH POLICY

### Malaysian Youth Council

Malaysia, according to United Nations statistics (1995), has a population of 20.7 million. Of that total, those aged 15-24 years account for 3.9 million (19.2 per cent), while those aged 25-39 years make up a further 4.9 million (23.4 per cent). The biggest group, comprising those aged under 15 years, totals 7.3 million (35.4 per cent).

### Background

Various youth development strategies and programmes have been implemented in the past few years by many concerned groups from various sectors. There are also several government agencies in Malaysia which are concerned with youth affairs, spearheaded by the Ministry of Youth and Sports (MYS) which was established in 1964. The youth organizations are led by the Malaysian Youth Council (MYC), established in 1948, which has a nationwide network of youth organizations. In addition, several NGOs and the private sector are concerned with youth development.

## The first National Youth Policy, 1995

In the early 1970s, the Malaysian Youth Council began advocating for a national youth policy. The main impetus for pursuing such a policy at that time was the lack of coordination among programmes for youth conducted by the various concerned sectors. This had resulted in duplication, competition, and uncoordinated implementation of youth-related activities by various governmental and non-governmental agencies.

There was a need for an overall national policy that would provide clear direction to link all the youth-related initiatives in the country. In order for the national youth policy to play such a role, it was necessary to generate a sense of ownership among those parties concerned with youth affairs regarding the youth policy. If the national policy was perceived more as the property of the Government rather than as the policy of all parties involved with youth affairs, it would not be effective. Therefore, the Council proposed the development of a new policy which would be recognized by all parties concerned, and which would strengthen the formulation of more effective youth programmes.

Discussions on the subject were held during numerous seminars and meetings up to 1979, when the National Youth Consultative Committee (NYCC) approved a Council proposal for the formulation of Malaysia's first National Youth Policy. The NYCC was established in the early 1970s as a formal mechanism for Government-NGO collaboration on youth-related matters. The NYCC meets twice a year and is chaired by the Minister of Youth and Sports. The members comprise, *inter alia*, representatives of the Ministry of Youth and Sports, the Malaysian Youth Council, ten other government agencies, as well as the State ministers who chair the 14 State committees for youth.

After extensive review by the concerned parties, the objectives, principles and strategies of the "National Youth Policy" were finally announced by the Government in 1985.

## The new National Youth "Development" Policy, 1996

In 1995, after a decade of implementing the National Youth Policy promulgated in 1985, there was a general view that the existing youth policy needed to be reviewed and revised accordingly. Consultations were held by both the Ministry of Youth ad Sports and the Malaysian Youth Council. At the same time, research was conducted by the academic sector to evaluate the effectiveness of the implementation of the policy.

A small closed-door "brainstorming" meeting among selected individuals, and chaired by the newly appointed Minister of Youth and Sports, was held at Langkawi in October 1995. The new Minister recognized the need to more actively involve the Malaysian Youth Council in policy-formulation. Prior to that meeting, the Ministry had circulated a draft of a "new youth policy". However, from the view point of the Council, the draft was no more than the addition and deletion of sentences to the existing policy; it was felt that the changes did not fully address the concerns of the Council. In addition, the Council was dissatisfied by the fact that it had not been consulted by the Ministry in the preparation process of the draft "new youth policy". The Council believed that the Ministry had a responsibility to consult the Council on major issues concerning youth in Malaysia, in its capacity as the partner organization in the joint secretariat of NYCC.

The views of the Malaysian Youth Council on the draft "new youth policy" were made at the above meeting. It was agreed that there was a need to revise the draft policy. The Secretary-General of the Council assumed the task of drafting an alternate proposal, which was entitled "The National Youth Development Policy". The proposal added an entirely new paradigm. Four major issues were taken into consideration in drafting the new policy: (a) defining the age range of youth (a consensus was reached that the main target group were those in the 15 to 24 year age bracket); (b) ensuring the full implementation of the policy so that it would really become effective; (c) placing greater emphasis on youth potentials rather than on their "problems"; and (d) making the policy more youth-centred and democratic by ensuring the full participation of youths in the planning and execution of youth programmes.

The proposed new policy was divided into two components: (a) a policy statement comprising the philosophy, the objectives, the main areas of operation and the target group; and (b) the strategies for implementation, covering 12 areas. These were: (i) the role of NYCC; (ii) professionalism among youth leaders, managers and workers; (iii) coordination between government agencies; (iv) the role of the private sector; (v) strengthening youth organizations and leadership; (vi) the role of other NGOs; (vii) the role of the media; (viii) education and training; (ix) youth activity centres; (x) research and development; (xi) evaluation and recognition; and (xii) finance.

To ensure sufficient involvement and participation by the various groups concerned with youth matters, the draft was thoroughly reviewed and discussed at meetings with representatives of various youth organizations and revised accordingly. The first draft was discussed at the Second National Youth Dialogue (organized annually by MYC as a forum for NGOs to discuss youth-related issues) on 3 December 1995, and at a special session of the MYC Executive Committee. It was then amended and the second draft was later discussed with MYS which accepted the MYC draft almost entirely. The third draft was later discussed with student leaders from three selected secondary schools and at two seminars involving university students, before being approved by the MYC Supreme Council on 18 December 1995. Then MYC presented the third draft to NYCC on 19 December 1995, when it was unanimously approved with a few amendments. A post-NYCC committee was appointed to finalize the draft. At the time of preparing this review paper in July 1996, the fourth draft was still under discussion. However, it was hoped that it would be tabled for Cabinet approval by the end of October 1996.

## B.    YOUTH PARTICIPATION FOR COMMUNITY DEVELOPMENT

Sarvodaya, an organization founded in 1958, applies the teaching of the Lord Buddha to community development. The name Sarvodaya is derived from two Sanskrit words meaning "universal" and "awakening", while Shramadana comes from the Sanskrit for "labour" and "sharing".

### Lanka Jatika Sarvodaya Shramadana Sangamaya, Sri Lanka

The objective of the organization is to provide opportunities for volunteers to engage in community development. This provides opportunities for youth to understand the socio-economic problems of the country and to learn the means of solving those problems, in accordance with the Sarvodaya philosophy.

Sarvodaya is a large organization that is currently active in some 8,000 villages in the country. There are 2,478 registered Sarvodaya Shramadana Societies in Sri Lanka. The organization employs a large full-time paid staff and many volunteers at all levels, although the current financial crisis has resulted in a significant reduction in the number of paid staff. Youth members of the organization, the core group of the volunteers, are aged between 16 and 25 years.

Thousands of young people in the Sarvodaya Shramadana movement of Sri Lanka offer their labour as a gift in rural areas. They help underprivileged people to build drinking water supplies and irrigation systems for their rice fields, roads to villages, schools and community centres for young people, and health and sanitation facilities. The youth workers, known as Gramadana workers, are provided with small allowances and bicycles by the programme, which trains them as facilitators in the local development process. The selection criteria for the workers ensures that they are of reputable character, have no affiliation with political party, have little or no family obligations, and possess a minimum secondary school education. Often those selected are already active volunteers in their villages, but the scheme ensures regular reinforcement of their training and experience through meetings and further training sessions.

Sarvodaya seeks to attract people, especially youths, and engage them actively as committed workers striving for a better society. In each village in which it is active, Sarvodaya seeks to recruit youths, involve them as workers in society, and provide them with training to adequately equip them to serve their country. Youths who have gone through training in different skills of village reconstruction serve as full-time workers. They inspire, learn from, educate, organize and work with the local people on a programme of self-development carved out by the community itself. Sarvodaya has over 30,000 trained village youths actively involved in improving the quality of life of their people.

Young people have launched practical programmes in more than 8,000 of a total 23,000 villages in Sri Lanka. The programmes support individuals, families and communities in realizing sustainable forms of development involving social, economic and political restructuring. Sarvodaya aims to network the village communities to make a national impact. Within this framework young people can participate in harmonizing the traditional and modern in an appropriate and practical manner, often over an extended period, until the village community becomes completely independent.

Part Three:

# Report of the Asia-Pacific Meeting on Human Resources Development for Youth, 22-26 October 1996, Beijing, Including the Beijing Statement on Human Resources Development for Youth in Asia and the Pacific

# Organization of the Meeting     I

## A.   BACKGROUND

The Asia-Pacific Meeting on Human Resources Development for Youth was held by the United Nations Economic and Social Commission for Asia and the Pacific (ESCAP) in Beijing from 22 to 26 October 1996. It was organized in cooperation with the All-China Youth Federation (ACYF), with financial assistance from the Government of China, the United Nations Population Fund (UNFPA) and the Christian Conference of Asia (CCA).

## B.   OBJECTIVES

The Meeting was convened in pursuance of Commission resolution 52/4 on "Promoting human resources development among youth in Asia and the Pacific". The specific objectives of the Meeting were to:

(1)    Review the regional youth situation, policies and programmes in the context of the *Jakarta Plan of Action on Human Resources Development in the ESCAP Region* and the World Programme of Action for Youth to the Year 2000 and Beyond, as adopted by the United Nations General Assembly in December 1995;

(2) Formulate proposals for regional cooperation in priority areas of youth human resources development; and

(3) Provide a regional input to the United Nations World Youth Forum to be held in Vienna in November 1996.

## C. ATTENDANCE

The Meeting was attended by representatives of the following ESCAP members and associate members: Bangladesh, Bhutan, Brunei Darussalam, Cambodia, China, Democratic People's Republic of Korea, Fiji, Guam, Hong Kong, India, Indonesia, Islamic Republic of Iran, Lao People's Democratic Republic, Macau, Maldives, Federated States of Micronesia, Myanmar, Nepal, Netherlands, Pakistan, Philippines, Republic of Korea, Sri Lanka, Thailand, Uzbekistan and Viet Nam.

Representatives from the following non-governmental organizations were present: Asian Youth Council (AYC), Malaysia; Christian Conference of Asia (CCA), Hong Kong; Centre for Development and Population Activities (CEDPA), USA; Commonwealth Youth Programme (CYP), India; Federation of Family Planning Associations of Malaysia (FFPAM), Malaysia; International Council of Adult Education (ICAE), India; Malaysian Youth Council (MYC), Malaysia; Mongolian Youth Federation (MYF), Mongolia; OISCA-International, Hong Kong Office; Pacific Youth Council (PYC), New Caledonia; Uppsala University, Sweden; World Youth Foundation (WYF), Malaysia; and Youth Challenge, Singapore.

Representatives of the following United Nations departments, bodies and specialized agencies were present: Department of Policy Coordination and Sustainable Development (DPCSD); International Labour Organization (ILO); United Nations Educational, Scientific and Cultural Organization (UNESCO); United Nations Population Fund (UNFPA); and World Health Organization (WHO).

## D. OPENING OF THE MEETING

Opening and welcoming statements were delivered on behalf of ESCAP and the All-China Youth Federation by Mr Liu Peng, President, All-China Youth Federation; and by the Director, Social Development Division, ESCAP.

## E.   ELECTION OF OFFICERS

The Meeting elected Mr. Liu Hehua, Deputy Secretary-General, ACYF, (China), chairperson; Ms. Salma Waheed, Federal Secretary, Ministry of Women's Development and Youth Affairs (Pakistan) and Mr. Ribomapil S. Holganza, Jr., Commissioner, National Youth Commission (Philippines), vice-chairpersons; and Mr. Paula Kunabuli, Director, Ministry of Youth, Employment and Opportunities, and Sports (Fiji), rapporteur.

## F.   ADOPTION OF AGENDA

The Meeting adopted the following agenda:

1.   Opening.

2.   Election of officers.

3.   Adoption of the agenda.

4.   The regional human resources development situation of youth in the context of:

   (a)   The Jakarta Plan of Action on Human Resources Development in the ESCAP Region;

   (b)   The World Programme of Action for Youth to the Year 2000 and Beyond.

5.   Policies and programmes to promote human resources development for youth:

   (a)   Education;

   (b)   Health;

   (c)   Employment.

6.   Mechanisms to promote participation in decision-making for youth.

7.   Regional cooperation to promote human resources development among youth.

8.   Field study.

9.   Adoption of the report.

# Summary of Deliberations  II

## A. THE REGIONAL HUMAN RESOURCES DEVELOPMENT SITUATION OF YOUTH IN THE CONTEXT OF:

### (i) The Jakarta Plan of Action on Human Resources Development in the ESCAP Region

The Director, Social Development Division, ESCAP, delivered a presentation on key issues for youth in the context of the Jakarta Plan of Action on Human Resources Development in the ESCAP region.

The presentation focused on: (1) the concept of "human resources development" as advocated in the Jakarta Plan of Action on Human Resources Development in the ESCAP Region; (2) the four key HRD issues affecting youth in the ESCAP region, namely, education, health, employment and participation; and (3) the results of a survey on youth policies conducted by ESCAP in accordance with a request in General Assembly resolution 47/85.

The presentation highlighted the need for regional cooperation in the promotion of human resources development of young people in Asia and the Pacific.  It was noted that while a number

of initiatives had been taken in the region during the course of the
decade following the 1985 International Youth Year, many countries
had yet to adopt youth policies and to establish youth focal-point
agencies. Sharing of experience in this regard could serve as a
valuable tool for the establishment and strengthening of youth
policies in the region. The possibilities for regional cooperation in
this field, particularly through networking of youth organizations,
both governmental and non-governmental, were considerable. The
participants at the Meeting were in a strategic position to pursue
such regional cooperation.

### (ii)  The World Programme of Action for Youth to the Year 2000 and Beyond

The Officer-in-Charge of the United Nations Youth Unit,
Department for Policy Coordination and Sustainable Development
(DPCSD), United Nations Headquarters, delivered a presentation on
the World Programme of Action for Youth to the Year 2000 and
Beyond, as adopted by the General Assembly in December 1995.

The World Programme of Action, *inter alia,* urges governments
to formulate and adopt an integrated national youth policy,
strengthen national coordinating mechanisms for and with youth,
and undertake national youth service programmes. At both the
regional and global levels, the Programme recommends two
platforms of action: one at the governmental level (consisting of
biennial United Nations meetings of ministers responsible for
youth) and the other assuming a tripartite – youth NGO, UN
system and IGO – character (consisting of biennial meetings of a
youth forum for non-governmental youth organizations, youth-
related bodies and agencies of the United Nations system, and
youth-related intergovernmental organizations).

The Meeting was informed that the United Nations was
currently finalizing plans for the organization of the World Youth
Forum of the United Nations System (second session), to be held
from 25 to 29 November 1996 at the United Nations Office at
Vienna. A proposal was also being discussed for a United Nations
Conference of Ministers responsible for Youth, possibly in July
1998, pursuant to the World Programme of Action for Youth.

The Meeting was further informed that a report was being
prepared on "Implementation of the World Programme of Action

for Youth to the Year 2000 and Beyond" for the next session of the General Assembly. National review meetings could be convened in selected countries of the ESCAP region in connection with the implementation process. It was mentioned that the United Nations Youth Fund, administered by DPCSD, could help this process, especially in the least developed countries of the region.

The open plenary discussion that ensued focused on:

- The need to reach an international consensus on the definition of "youth" in order to ensure more target-oriented policies for young people.

- The need to promote youth policies with more comprehensive objectives.

- The need for collaboration among government agencies and among NGOs as well as between government agencies, NGOs and private-sector entities in the development and implementation of youth policies and programmes.

- The possibility of developing a system of youth development indicators, given the lack of information on the status of youth in the Asia-Pacific region.

## B. POLICIES AND PROGRAMMES TO PROMOTE HUMAN RESOURCES DEVELOPMENT FOR YOUTH

### (i) Education

The President of the International Council of Adult Education, in her presentation under this agenda item, stressed the role of education as a means to empower young people. The purpose of education should be beyond employment generation; it should be used to build democracy, participation in governance and the building of civil society. Youth education was therefore a major instrument for constructive change. Youth education was a binding factor in achieving progress in the areas of health, employment and participation.

The Meeting noted that much progress had been made towards attaining universal literacy in many countries of the region. However, unacceptably high levels of illiteracy still existed among youth, particularly girls, young women and disadvantaged groups, in many parts of the region. Some delegations observed that fundamental socio-economic and cultural factors were the cause of the low levels of literacy in those countries.

The role of education for all in promoting gender sensitization was also discussed. It was agreed that education could provide positive contributions towards achieving that goal. Various experiences at the national level were exchanged by the participants.

Some participants stressed the need to review the relevance and quality of education continuously in order to ensure that the full potential of youth would be developed. In that connection, it was observed that mismatches in educational levels and skills orientations between job seekers and job providers had contributed to youth unemployment and underemployment in some countries.

### (ii)  Health

The Senior Technical Officer; Education, Communication and Youth Branch; Technical and Evaluation Division, UNFPA, in his keynote statement under this agenda item, provided an overview of priority issues for youth in the field of health, particularly reproductive health, including family planning and sexual health, within the context of the international consensus achieved at the 1994 Cairo International Conference on Population and Development and the 1995 Beijing Fourth World Conference on Women, and as contained in the 1996 World Programme of Action for Youth.

He noted that young people needed accurate, age-specific information related to their reproductive health, which would help to deter risky behaviour and promote sound family life. Providing that information to young people within the family, within the community and among peers, as well as using such communications channels as teachers and the media, was discussed. Some measures taken by countries facing the spread of AIDS were also covered.

The Meeting noted with concern that sexual abuse (rape and incest) and sexual exploitation (trafficking, pornography and prostitution) had affected many young people, particularly girls, in the region. It was agreed that Governments, in partnership with NGOs, should take effective steps for combating those problems, both at the national and international levels. One participant noted that in the context of those problems, the term "youth" encompassed children, adolescents and young people up to the age of 24 years.

It was noted that some countries in the region had recorded only limited success in achieving satisfactory basic health standards for young people. That problem was in part related to the unsatisfactory nutritional levels of youth in some countries. The lack of doctors and medical services in rural areas, and the need for specific approaches to address the health needs of young people in those areas, was also highlighted.

## (iii)   Employment

The Executive President of Youth Challenge, Singapore, in his presentation under this agenda item, reviewed the work of his organization in providing youth with employment opportunities. Those programmes had been carried out in close cooperation with the private sector of his country. Through the use of innovative approaches to reach the target group, the programme had achieved considerable success.

The Meeting observed that in many countries, unemployment among youth had been considerably higher than for other parts of the population. In countries with such a labour surplus, the educational system had been burdened with the responsibility of providing young people with skills, even where the labour market clearly could not absorb them. In view of that problem, which was in some countries associated with high rates of unemployment among educated youth, various ways and means of coordinating educational curricula labour market requirements were highlighted. Some participants called for the extensive involvement of the private sector in order to address that problem.

High unemployment rates in rural areas had, throughout much of the region, led to the migration of young people to urban areas in search of jobs. In some cases, it had also led to emigration of young workers to other countries. The provision of youth employment-skills trainers at the rural community level was highlighted as a possible solution to the problem.

## C. PARTICIPATION

The Secretary General of the Malaysian Youth Council, in his presentation under this agenda item, focused on the contribution of his organization in the formulation of the new National Youth Policy of Malaysia. The Policy contains two components: a policy statement comprising the philosophy, objectives, main areas of operation and target groups; and an implementation strategy covering 12 areas. They are: (1) role of the national youth consultative council; (2) professionalism among youth leaders, managers and workers; (3) coordination among government agencies; (4) role of the private sector; (5) strengthening of youth organizations and leadership; (6) role of other NGOs; (7) role of the media; (8) education and training; (9) youth activity centres; (10) research and development; (11) evaluation; and (12) financing.

The presentation and ensuing discussion highlighted the following conditions for the formulation of an effective national youth policy:

- The need for meaningful participation of all concerned government agencies, NGOs and youth leaders in the policy formulation stage, through the establishment of consultative mechanisms.

- The need for fomulation of comprehensive policy objectives and principles.

- The need to define a more focused age range for youth.

- The need to consider youth as a "potential", rather than as a "problem".

- The need to make national development policies more youth-oriented and democratic by ensuring the participation of youth at all stages of programme planning, implementation and evaluation.

- The need to incorporate planning, marketing, implementation and evaluation of youth development programmes in the policy process.

## D. REGIONAL COOPERATION TO PROMOTE HUMAN RESOURCES DEVELOPMENT FOR YOUTH

The Meeting divided into four workshops to develop specific proposals for regional cooperation to promote HRD for youth in Asia and the Pacific in the following areas: education; health; employment; and participation.

The following participants served as chairpersons and rapporteurs of the respective workshops:

### Education:

| | |
|---|---|
| Chairperson: | Ms Shagufta Alizai (Pakistan) |
| Rapporteur: | Mr Zakariyya Hussein (Maldives) |

### Health:

| | |
|---|---|
| Chairperson: | Dr Yongyud Wongpiromsarn (Thailand) |
| Rapporteur: | Dr Yee Thiam Sun (Malaysia) |

### Employment:

| | |
|---|---|
| Chairperson: | Mr Leo Rama (Philippines) |
| Rapporteur: | Mr H. M. Gunasekera (Sri Lanka) |

### Participation:

| | |
|---|---|
| Chairperson: | Mr A. Z. Iskandar (Indonesia) |
| Rapporteur: | Mr Saifuddin Abdullah (Malaysia) |

Each of the four workshops reviewed the major issues in its area, as discussed during Plenary. It prioritized those issues and formulated two proposals which it considered of particular relevance for regional cooperation to promote HRD for youth in Asia and the Pacific.

The titles of the proposals, classified by subject area, are as follows:

### Education:

- Promoting continuing education through distance learning

- Improving the quality of secondary, technical and vocational education and training

*Health:*

- Promoting reproductive health of youth
- Eliminating sexual abuse and sexual exploitation of youth

*Employment:*

- Preparing youth for the world of work
- Matching youth education and skills with employment opportunities

*Participation:*

- Developing youth participation indicators (YPIs)
- Strengthening national youth coordination mechanisms

## E. FIELD STUDY

A field study was organized by the All-China Youth Federation for participants to visit a number of skills development programmes for youth in the vicinity of Beijing, including the Centre for Scientific and Agricultural Experiment, the Adult Educational School and the East Asian Aluminum Cooperation in Zhang Jia Wan Township, Tongxian County.

## F. ADOPTION OF THE REPORT

The Meeting adopted its report and the Beijing Statement on Human Resources Development for Youth in Asia and the Pacific on 26 October 1996.

# Beijing Statement on Human Resources Development for Youth in Asia and the Pacific

We, the representatives of member and associate member governments and representatives of non-governmental organizations attending the Asia-Pacific Meeting on Human Resources Development for Youth (Beijing, 22-26 October 1996), transmit this statement to the World Youth Forum of the United Nations System. We transmit this statement as a contribution from Asia and the Pacific to the evolution of a global vision of the role of youth in development in the twenty-first century.

In considering the challenges for human resources development for youth in Asia and the Pacific, we took as our point of departure the *Jakarta Plan of Action on Human Resources Development in the ESCAP Region*, which identifies youth as a priority target group for human resources development in terms of each of the three interdependent components comprising the human resources development process: investment in human resources to enhance productive capabilities; utilization of those human resources to produce increased output; and consumption of the resulting outputs to improve the quality of life.

We were also guided by the *World Programme of Action for Youth to the Year 2000 and Beyond*, which contains proposals for integrated action to address more effectively the problems of young people and enhance their participation in development. In reviewing the specific priority areas for youth identified in that global instrument, we considered four areas of special concern for human resources development in the Asian and Pacific context: education, health, employment and participation.

Our discussions on each of those priority areas resulted in a series of practical proposals for action for possible implementation by the year 2000, each focusing on regional cooperation to promote human resources development among youth in Asia and the Pacific. The major proposals are summarized below:

*Education:*

> *Promoting continuing education through distance learning* – This proposal would target marginalized and out-of-school youth, particularly girls, young women and disadvantaged groups, to provide basic life skills, including literacy and numeracy skills, through continuing education, applying distance learning technologies. The main activities would include the sharing of national experiences in distance education technologies and curriculums, regional networking of distance education institutes, and the establishment of a regional database on continuing education through distance education.

> *Improving the quality of secondary, technical and vocational education and training* – This proposal would seek to enhance acquired competencies to empower youth for effective participation in the world of work and community life. The main activities would include curriculum development and teacher training through curricular research, teacher-trainers' exchange programmes and information sharing.

*Health:*

*Promoting reproductive health of youth* – The proposal would pursue a series of youth-oriented reproductive health promotion activities, involving the participation of youth, including: situation studies on reproductive health among youth; sensitization and awareness promotion among policy makers, programme implementors and youth organizations; exchange of experiences on successful approaches; capacity strengthening of regional and national resource centres; and training of health professionals.

*Eliminating sexual abuse and sexual exploitation of youth* – The proposal would, involving the participation of youth, undertake a series of activities to combat the sexual abuse and sexual exploitation of youth, including: research to determine the current status of the problem in the region; sensitization and awareness promotion among policy makers, youth organizations and the tourism industry; exchange of experiences on successful approaches in combating the problem; training of health providers to meet the special needs of the victims; promotion of gainful alternatives for the victims and potential victims; and strengthening of the capacity of regional and national centres for the prevention and elimination of the problem.

*Employment:*

*Preparing youth for the world of work* – This proposal would introduce and strengthen career and vocational education and counseling programmes for youth and explore options for career and vocational tracking of youth within the educational process. The main activities would include: research studies on alternative career and vocational tracking systems through needs assessment surveys among youth; development and implementation of training-of-trainers programmes on career education and counseling for youth leaders as well as for government and NGO youth personnel; cooperation between educational institutions and the private sector to promote the concepts of "earning while learning" and "learning while earning"; and development of curricular and learning materials for career education and vocational guidance and counseling.

*Matching youth education and skills with employment opportunities* – This proposal would seek to ensure that the employment skills imparted to youth fit the employment opportunities arising within the changing labour market. The main activities would include the sharing of national experiences regarding labour-market clearing mechanisms; promotion of information exchange on partnership relationships between the private and government sectors for promoting youth self-employment opportunities; a regional conference to develop a plan of action for promoting and supporting youth entrepreneurship; and establishment of a regional revolving fund to support income-generating activities for youth.

## Participation:

*Developing youth participation indicators (YPIs)* – This proposal would develop a series of youth participation indicators (YPIs) to facilitate the analysis of, and thereby promote, youth participation in the planning, implementation and evaluation of national youth and related policies. Among the main activities would be: the formulation of an agreed list of YPIs; survey and analysis of national situations with respect to those indicators; exchange of information on national experiences; and national workshops and regional meetings to monitor the YPIs and consider appropriate response.

*Strengthening national youth coordination mechanisms* – This proposal would provide regional support to the establishment and strengthening of national youth coordination mechanisms as the institutional cornerstone of action to promote youth participation in decision-making and development. Among the major activities will be: technical assistance to establish and strengthen in each Asian and Pacific country and area a national inter-ministerial coordinating mechanism, operating in close association with a national non-governmental youth council or committee; regular dissemination of information on national youth programmes in the region; a series of national and subregional workshops of national youth coordinating mechanisms to promote regional cooperation in the field of youth participation in development and to review the implementation of the World Programme of Action for

Youth, and a regional intergovernmental meeting, with the participation of both governments, NGOs and other concerned bodies, to review the implementation of the proposals for action adopted by this Meeting as well as to review progress in the implementation of the World Programme of Action for Youth.

We, the representatives of member and associate member governments and representatives of non-governmental organizations concerned with youth in the Asian and the Pacific region, commend these proposals to the attention of the World Youth Forum of the United Nations System as practical means of energizing increased regional, inter-regional and global cooperation in pursuit of human resources development of youth into the twenty-first century.

*26 October 1996*

# Bibliography

Advocates for Youth, *Passages*, Washington D.C. October/ November 1995.

Commonwealth Secretariat. Approaching youth policy: cross-reference policy development. London, Commonwealth Secretariat Publications, 1990.

_____ Youth policy and its implication; based on the recommendations of the regional policy consultation. London, Commonwealth Secretariat Publications, 1992.

Commonwealth Youth Programme. *In Common* (Issues 12-13). The United Kingdom of Great Britain and Northern Ireland, Commonwealth Secretariat, 1994.

_____ Rural Youth and Participatory Development. The United Kingdom, Commonwealth Secretariat.

Commonwealth Youth Programme Asia Centre. Asian Region Seminar on Commonwealth Youth in a Changing World: Future Directions. Kuala Lumpur, 2-8 April 1995.

_____ Youth policy and its implementation; based on the recommendations of the Regional Policy Consultation. Chandigarh, India, 1992.

Hemrich, Gunter. Integration of population education into programmes for out-of-school rural youth: a review of pilot activities in Africa, Asia and Latin America. Food and Agriculture Organization of the United Nations), January 1996. (INT/92/P94).

Indian Committee of Youth Organizations. *Youth Information.* New Delhi, October 1994 and March 1996.

The International Council on Management of Population Programmes. Report of the Workshop on Innovative Approaches in Youth Reproductive Health Programmes, Melaka, Malaysia, 1-4 June 1995.

International Labour Organization, Regional Office for Asia and the Pacific. ILO activities for youth in the Asia/Pacific region; paper presented at the International Meeting on Establishment and Development of National Machineries for Youth, Bangkok, 8-12 November 1989.

_____ Female Asian migrants: a growing but increasingly vulnerable workforce. ILO press release, Bangkok, 5 February 1996.

International Planned Parenthood Federation. Planned Parenthood Challenges 1996/1. Advocacy for reproductive health: dialogue challenges overview responses. International Planned Parenthood Federation, London, 1996.

International Youth Press Service. *The Youth Round Up.* Copenhagen, October 1995 and December 1995.

International Youth Consultation on Social Development. Papers distributed at the meeting. Idroaettens Hus, Copenhagen, 3-5 March 1995.

Kato, Mayumi. Municipality and youth partnership. Paper presented at the Conference on Youth and Urban Living, Kuala Lumpur, 9-11 April 1996.

Khare, Shiv. Making youth ministries effective across the range of important youth concerns and needs; paper presented at the Commonwealth Youth Ministers Meeting, incorporating the Commonwealth Youth Affairs Council, Maldives, 10-12 May 1992.

_____ International Meeting on the Role of the Family in the Socialization of Youth: background paper on issues and problems related to the interactive roles of the family and youth in society. Presented at the Interregional Meeting on the Role of the Family in the Socialization of Youth, Beijing, 31 May to 4 June 1993.

_____ Adolescent reproductive health programme for non-student youth in Asia: an overview. Paper presented at the Regional Workshop on Innovative Approaches in Youth Reproductive Health Programmes, Malaysia, June 1995.

Ministry of Youth and Sports, Malaysia. National Youth Policy, Kuala Lumpur, 1985.

_____ Guidelines for Rakan Muda Programme Development, Kuala Lumpur, 28 December 1994.

Mohammud, Asha. Adolescent reproductive health and fertility in Africa, the Middle East and South Asia. April 1993.

National Clearinghouse for Youth Studies. *Youth Studies Australia.* August 1991, 10:3; Winter 1995, 14:2; March 1996, 15:1. National Clearinghouse for Youth Studies, Hobart, Tasmania.

Pyvis, David. "Is youth policy really new?," *Youth Studies Australia.* Autumn 1992, 11:1. National Clearinghouse for Youth Studies, Hobart, Tasmania.

Seah, Chee-Meow. "Human resources development policies and programmes for youth and programmes for youth in Asia and the Pacific". *Asia Youth Magazine.* 8 January 1991.

United Nations. Guidelines for further planning and suitable follow-up in the field of youth. United Nations General Assembly fortieth session, New York, 1985.

_____ National youth policies in developing countries. New York, 1985. (ST/ESA/166).

_____ Statistical charts and indicators of the situation of youth, 1970-1990. New York, 1992.

_____ The global situation of youth in the 1990s: trends and prospects. New York, 1993. (ST/CSDHA/21).

_____ The family and youth: issues, problems and opportunities. Occasional Papers Series, No. 11. Vienna, 1994.

_____ *Youth Information Bulletin.* 1994, 1:83; 1995, 2:87. New York.

_____ *United Nations Youth Newsletter.* 1995, issues 13 and 14. New York.

_____ Information package distributed at Youth Day: Fourth World Conference on Women. Beijing, 11 September 1995.

United Nations Development Programme. Human Development Report, 1995, New York. Oxford University Press, 1995.

United Nations Economic and Social Council. World Programme of Action for Youth to the Year 2000 and Beyond, New York, 16 October 1995. (E/1995/123).

United Nations Economic and Social Commission for Asia and the Pacific. Report of the Seminar on Human Resources Development Policies and Programmes for Youth in the ESCAP Region, 15-19 October 1990, Inchon, Republic of Korea. United Nations, New York 1991. (ST/ESCAP/971).

_____ Trends, patterns and implications of rural-urban migration in India, Nepal and Thailand. Asian Population Studies Series No. 138. United Nations, New York, 1995.

_____ Strengthening of regional cooperation in human resources development in Asia and the Pacific: with special reference to the social implications of sustainable economic growth. United Nations, New York, 1995. (ST/ESCAP/1467).

_____ Working with women in poverty: nine innovative approaches submitted for the ESCAP HRD Award (1995 edition). United Nations, New York, 1996. (ST/ESCAP/1648).

_____ Functional literacy for women's empowerment in South Asia. United Nations, New York, 1995.

_____ New urban contract needed to stall city crisis in Asia and the Pacific. ESCAP press release G/10/96, Bangkok, 5 March 1996.

United Nations Educational, Scientific and Cultural Organization. Final report; Advisory Committee on Regional Co-operation in Education in Asia and the Pacific, Seventh Session, Kuala Lumpur, 14-17 June 1993). UNESCO Principal Regional Office for Asia and the Pacific, Bangkok, 1993.

_____ Final report; Sixth Regional Conference of Ministers of Education and those Responsible for Economic Planning in Asia and the Pacific. Organized by UNESCO with the co-operation of ESCAP, Kuala Lumpur, 21-24 June 1993. UNESCO, Paris, October 1993. (ED/MD/97).

_____ Development of education in Asia and the Pacific: issues and prospects. First Meeting of the Intergovernmental Regional Committee on Education in Asia and the Pacific, Bangkok, 24-26 June 1996. UNESCO Principal Regional Office for Asia and the Pacific, Bangkok, June 1996. (PROAP-96/EDCOM1/4).

_____ Development of education in Asia and the Pacific: a statistical review. Paper presented at the First Meeting of the Intergovernmental Regional Committee on Education in Asia and the Pacific, 24-26 June 1996. UNESCO Principal Regional Office for Asia and the Pacific, Bangkok, June 1996. (PROAP-96/EDCOM1/5).

_____ Adolescence education: physical aspects. Population Education Programme Service: Module One. UNESCO Principal Regional Office for Asia and the Pacific, Bangkok, 1991.

_____ Adolescence education: social aspects. Population Education Programme Service: Module Two. UNESCO Principal Regional Office for Asia and the Pacific, Bangkok, 1991.

_____ Adolescence education: sex roles. Population Education Programme Service: Module Three. UNESCO Principal Regional Office for Asia and the Pacific, Bangkok, 1991.

_____ Adolescence education: sexually transmitted diseases. Population Education Programme Service: Module Four. UNESCO Principal Regional Office for Asia and the Pacific, Bangkok, 1991.

_____ Asia and the Pacific Educational Innovation Development in Action; report to the First Meeting of the Intergovernmental Regional Committee on Education in Asia and the Pacific, 24-26 June 1996. UNESCO Principal Regional Office for Asia and the Pacific, Bangkok, 1996.

_____ Asia and the Pacific Programme of Educational Innovation for Development. Innovative education for promoting the enterprise competencies of children and youth: report of a planning meeting, Bangkok, 11-15 December 1989. UNESCO Principal Regional Office for Asia and the Pacific, 1990.

_____ Asia and the Pacific Programme of Educational Innovation for Development. Education for nurturing enterprising abilities: report of a finalization meeting on the Asia and the Pacific Programme of Educational Innovation for Development Joint Innovative Project on Education for Promoting the Enterprise Competencies of Children and Youth, Bangkok. UNESCO Principal Regional Office for Asia and the Pacific, 1992.

United Nations Children's Fund. The Progress of Nations; the nations of the world ranked according to their achievements in child health, nutrition, education, family planning, and progress for humanity. UNICEF, New York, 1994.

World Assembly of Youth. World Youth Data Sheet 95. World Assembly of Youth, Copenhagen, 1995.

World Bank. World development indicators. World Development Report 1995: Workers in an Integrating World. World Bank, Washington D.C., 1995.

World Health Organization. The World Health Report 1995. Bridging the gaps; report of the Director-General. World Health Organization, Geneva, 1995.

_____ Position paper: health in social development. World Summit for Social Development, Copenhagen, March 1995. World Health Organization, Geneva, 1995.